How to Excel in Medical School

Second Edition

How to Excel in Medical School

Second Edition

Norma Susswein Saks, Ed.D.

**Assistant Dean for Educational Programs and
Director, Cognitive Skills Program
University of Medicine and Dentistry of New Jersey-
Robert Wood Johnson Medical School
Piscataway, NJ**

Mark Ari Saks, M.D., M.P.H.

**Resident in Emergency Medicine
Temple University Hospital
Philadelphia, PA**

J&S

J&S Publishing Company Inc., Alexandria, Virginia

J&S

Composition and Layout: Ronald C. Bohn, Ph.D.
Editing and Cover Design: Kurt E. Johnson, Ph.D.
Printing Supervisor: Robert Perotti, Jr.
Printing: Goodway Graphics of Virginia, Inc., Springfield, VA

Library of Congress Catalog Card Number 2003109072

ISBN 1-888308-15-X

Dedication

For all medical students who work so hard to learn so much in preparing for careers of helping and caring.

For Richard, Brad, and Emily.

Acknowledgements

The authors would like to acknowledge Drs. Carolina M. Zingale, Ph.D. and Daniel G. Stewart, M.D., the co-authors of the first edition and Grace Bingham, Ed. D., who provided the foundation for the second edition of *How to Excel in Medical School*. Special thanks to Carlotta Marino, without whose help this project could not have succeeded, to Dr. Robert Lebeau, Ed.D., and Emily Kirschner, M.D., for their helpful suggestions, and to all those who helped teach us about medicine and medical education. We are grateful to Dr. Kurt E. Johnson for giving a mother and son the special opportunity to write this book together. We also thank our family for their ongoing encouragement and support. We would like to acknowledge the use of the excellent illustrations by Diane Abeloff, A.M.I. published in *Medical Art: Graphics for Use*, Williams and Wilkins, Baltimore, 1982.

Disclaimer

The clinical information presented in this book is accurate for the purposes of general discussion of methods of achieving success in medical school but in no way should be used to treat patients or substituted for modern clinical training. Proper diagnosis and treatment of patients requires comprehensive evaluation of all symptoms, careful monitoring for adverse responses to treatment and assessment of the long-term consequences of therapeutic intervention.

CONTENTS

INTRODUCTION

Why a book about studying in medical school? While most medical students have been highly successful throughout their academic careers, in elementary school, high school, college, and even graduate school, many find medical school challenging. The vast majority of medical students develop effective study methods through a trial and error process and get through school. But often it can be a slow and frustrating process. This book is intended to guide you and help you to develop the learning skills you will need. Learning and applying these strategies will help get you off to a good start in your basic science courses and ease your learning throughout medical school and in your career as a physician.

Why Is Medical School So Hard?

When you matriculate into medical school, before too long you will learn that the level of competition has changed dramatically from what you have likely been accustomed to. In college, you were probably at or near the top of the class academically. You wouldn't have gotten into medical school otherwise. In medical school you may find yourself in the middle of the group, struggling to meet self-imposed standards for outstanding performance. This will require significant psychological adjustment. Most medical students make this adjustment by realizing that they have untapped abilities and by achieving a more sophisticated understanding of their skills and potentials.

There is very little information presented in medical school that is conceptually more difficult than that presented in your undergraduate science courses. This may sound surprising since medical school is considered by many to be the most difficult educational experience of all. So, what is it, besides the psychological adjustment, that makes medical school hard?

Volume of Information: Details, Details, Details

Students must assimilate an incredible amount of information in four short years. Remember, now you are a novice but in four years you will be a medical doctor! In medical school, information is presented at a rapid pace, and there appears to be an overwhelming number of tiny details to be assimilated quickly. The number of details for which you are responsible and the rate at which you are expected to learn them are the two primary reasons why medical school is so challenging.

In college, you often had the time to learn everything assigned. You sat down and worked through a list of tasks to completion, a method considered content-driven studying because the amount of studying you did was based on how much information you needed to know. (**Figure I.1**)

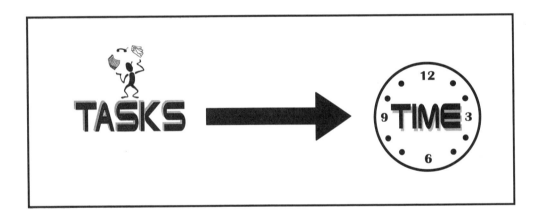

Figure I.1

In medical school, there is far more information to learn than there is time to learn it. There is no way to learn all the information to a level of mastery. This often creates some anxiety for students who have been used to getting through everything in as much depth as necessary. In medical school, you will need to sit down and look at a list of study tasks, and then decide how many of them can be done in the time available before each examination. The decisions about studying thus become time-driven, determined not by the amount of information, which may as well be infinite, but by the time one has, which is all too finite (**Figure I.2**). Shifting from content-driven to time-driven studying can be difficult, but this shift is crucial for success in medical school.

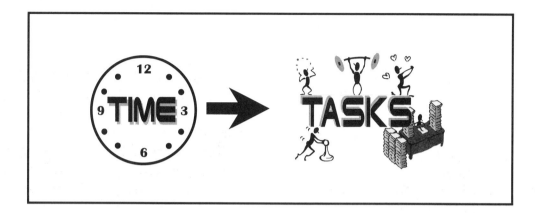

Figure I.2

What Makes Medical School So Different?

The Classes

Unlike college, you will not be able to choose your medical school classes or your medical school teachers. All medical students learn a core curriculum that includes Gross Anatomy, Microscopic Anatomy (Histology), Biochemistry, Microbiology, Physiology, etc. Lectures are usually presented to the whole class and therefore, there is typically no choice of teachers or class times.

The Instructors

Most of your teachers are likely to be researchers (Ph.D.'s) or clinicians (M.D.'s) for whom teaching may not be a top priority. Their rewards, promotions, and tenure are based only a little (and perhaps not at all) on their effectiveness as teachers. In addition, they may not have had much training about the most effective ways to keep you interested and involved in classes. It is likely that their selection as instructors is based on their abilities as scientists and/or clinical investigators. There will often be many lecturers for each course, which can lead to the feeling that courses (and examinations) are disjointed. The adage "Too many cooks spoil the broth" can unfortunately be true. Some of your teachers will be wonderful and you will wish they could present every lecture. Others will make you wonder why they are professors.

The Road to Success

In most learning situations, it seems that bright people can succeed by using just about any study strategy as long as it is applied diligently and consistently. Not so for medical school. Some medical students study endlessly, only to find themselves getting poor grades on examinations. The strategies which may have been useful for them previously may now be inefficient and ineffective. Therefore, it is essential to incorporate strategies that enhance learning so that your investment (the effort you put in) will give you a better return (more effective learning, higher grades and greater satisfaction). Certain kinds of studying will bring you a better return than others. By applying the techniques presented in this book, you will make it through medical school successfully, with better performance and with less stress.

PART I

GENERAL STRATEGIES

CHAPTER 1

THE BASICS

Effective Learning

Effective learning is active.

When you think back, much of the learning you did in kindergarten was active. You built with blocks to learn about gravity, molded clay to learn about shapes, poured sand to learn about conservation of matter, and cooked food to learn about measurement. However, as you moved through school, the opportunity for active learning, for hands-on experiences, was diminished. Unfortunately, much of the learning in secondary school, college, and yes, medical school, is presented in a lecture format with you as the passive recipient of information. In medical school, the basic science years often fall prey to a lecture-at-the-students-and-send-them-away-to-memorize-the-material format. This passive approach is ineffective for promoting optimum retention, synthesis, and mastery of the material.

Effective learning is self-directed.

It is essential for medical students as future physicians to become self-directed learners, to make decisions about what to learn, how much to learn, and for what purpose. Medicine is a field in which new information, based on new research findings and new discoveries, is continuously being generated. This means that all medical students will need to carry their learning skills with them throughout their medical careers. As practicing physicians, you will still need to keep learning and assimilating information at a brisk pace. You will need to enhance the skills that best promote lifelong, self-directed, efficient learning. This ongoing learning activity is required if you are to stay up-to-date. Such a habit of continuous learning will make you a better doctor for your patients.

Effective learning is aggressive.

Aggressive learning means mastering material deliberately. To be an aggressive learner means synthesizing material, considering the similarities and differences between ideas, between concepts, and between facts, and developing the ability to make predictions about upcoming material. To learn aggressively, keep questions like these in mind as you study:

1. What do I know and how does it all fit together?
2. What else do I need to know, and what is the fastest way I can learn it?
3. What do I expect to learn next?
4. What is the best use of my time right now?

Remember, when you are studying and acquiring new material in medical school, you are acquiring a database of information that will require continuous fine tuning. Concepts mastered today will either be useful for the rest of your practice life or will become hopelessly outmoded. It will be your responsibility to keep that which is useful, discard that which is outmoded, and acquire new information that is relevant to your particular interests and that will improve your patient management skills in your practice. This process requires aggressive learning on your part.

Effective learning requires self-monitoring.

Self-monitoring involves maintaining an awareness of everything you do that affects your learning. It entails examining your efficiency and effectiveness as a student with the goal of improving upon what you are doing. Self-monitoring requires disciplined self-questioning and self-evaluation. While there are basic principles and strategies for studying in medical school, there are no universally applicable formulas for success. You will need to decide what to study, when to study, where to study, how to study, and when to stop studying. Self-monitoring is a key to success in medical school and will be a recurring theme throughout this book. Developing self-monitoring skills will heighten your psychological self-awareness and provide you with a more objective, accurate assessment of your strengths and weaknesses.

Setting Priorities

So much to learn, so little time. Students who decide they are going to try to learn everything in medical school set themselves up to become inordinately stressed, highly anxious, and consequently less successful. Trying to read or memorize every detail from start to finish (called linear learning) may have worked well in college when finishing everything was actually possible. However, medical students who use a linear approach often run out of time before a test, and the untouched material cannot be utilized on the examination at all.

It is essential to set priorities for what you are going to learn to survive in the time-driven environment of medical school. This means determining a hierarchy for the order in which you are going to learn the material. That way if you do run out of time, you will still get the best return for the effort you have put in.

An effective technique for acquiring material is to build from a frame which is illustrated in **Figures 1.1, 1.2, and 1.3**. This method involves making several passes through the material, each for a different purpose. The following steps outline this approach:

1. **Build an overview or frame**. Get a general sense of the material by first learning the major concepts, the big categories, the major divisions, or ideas. (Specific strategies for this step, Previewing, are described in Chapter 2.)

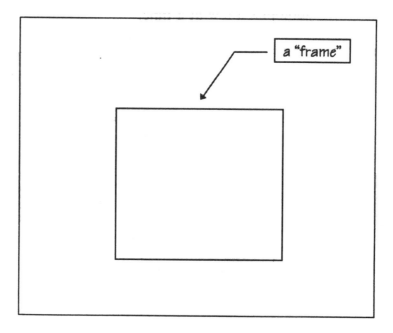

Figure 1.1

2. **Add successive layers of detail.** Include subtopics a few at a time.

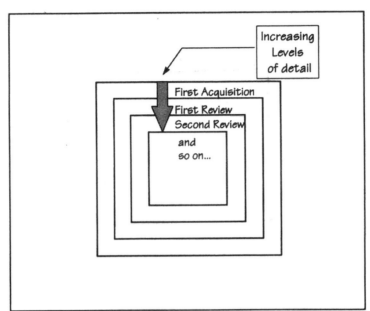

Figure 1.2

3. **Continue to acquire layers of details.** It is likely you will never get to the center of the frame, knowing it all. However, you will get far enough in each topic to answer most examination questions correctly.

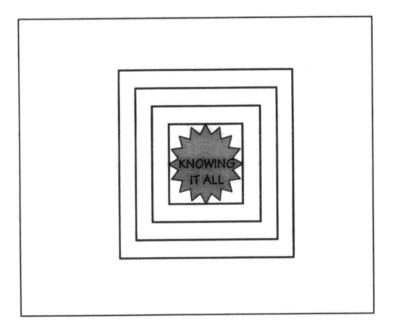

Figure 1.3

Students are often amazed at their ability to predict examination questions even when they have not learned all those details. For example, consider this information:

Heart muscle is called self-firing because it contracts to cause the beating of the heart without any external stimulation.

Based on this knowledge, you should be able to answer the following test question:

A patient's EKG reveals two P waves instead of the usual one (the wave associated with atrial contraction) for every QRS complex (which coincides with ventricular contraction). This phenomenon is MOST likely due to which of the following:

    (A)   Increased excitation from the vagus nerve
    (B)   Increased excitation from the phrenic nerve
    (C)   A problem in the feedback loop of innervation from the CNS
    (D)   A block in the conduction system within the heart muscle

You should have chosen the correct answer D because options A, B, and C all involve communication between the outside and the inside of the heart. Having learned the general concept, that no outside external stimulation is necessary, makes D the only correct answer.

The Process of Learning: Acquisition, Maintenance, and Proficiency

As a physician, you will need to have at your command an incredible amount of information. You will need to catalogue this information in a way that will allow you to access it quickly and accurately. Medical students are often unaware of how the task of retaining such vast amounts of information is best accomplished. The student who tries to retain information by rote memorization or brute force (studying ineffectively for long hours) will be at a disadvantage later. Information studied this way is not remembered well for a long time. Knowledge about the learning process, the three Stages of Learning, and the effective strategies associated with each, will help you become a better learner, a better examination taker, and ultimately a better physician.

Acquisition is the first stage in the learning process.

In medical school much of the information you acquire will come from textbooks and other written sources of information, from lectures, lab work, computers, and clinical experiences. The major goal of acquisition is to be certain that the material you study is understood. Strategies for learning during the acquisition stage will be described in the next chapter. The principles to keep in mind as you are first acquiring information are:

1. **Separate what you know from what is new:** The time-driven nature of medical school makes it important to avoid relearning something that you already know. One of your goals when setting study priorities will be to pass over information that you have learned previously to get to unfamiliar topics.

2. **Learn for recall, not recognition:** Do you know what a penny looks like? Most people would answer "Of course!" when asked this question. However, when asked to recall the face of a penny in order to draw it, people typically have a great deal of difficulty. (You may want to give it a try and see how you fare.) In a research study (Nickerson and Adams, 1979), participants were able to draw an average of three of the eight features on the face of a penny. You may conclude that although it is difficult to draw a penny, it would be easy to recognize it and select the correct version from among several incorrect versions (a multiple choice format). Before reading further see if you can identify the real penny in **Figure 1.4**.

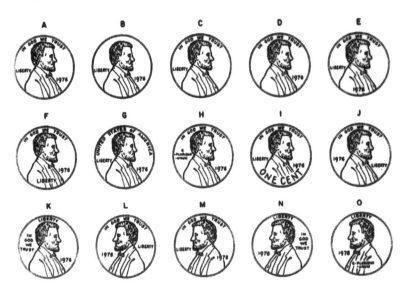

Figure 1.4

From: Nickerson, R.S. & Adams, M.J. (1979). Long-term memory for a common object. *Cognitive Psychology*, 11, p. 171. Reprinted by permission of Academic Press.

Answer **A** is the correct choice. If you answered incorrectly, or were uncertain about your response, you are not alone. Less than 50% of the participants in the study were able to select the correct version of the penny.

This example should make you think about how you will know when you really know something and are ready for an examination. Many students say they can feel when they are ready for a test but beware because feelings of knowledge are not enough. For example, most people feel they know what a penny looks like because it is familiar. It is risky to depend on feelings of familiarity and expect that these will translate into success on examinations. Instead, to insure that you know something, you must aim to recall it on your own from memory. This means that if you plan to study for the penny test, you should do more than just look at it again and again. You should practice drawing the penny from memory until you can draw it accurately. Self-testing is critical. It will enhance your confidence and accuracy on examinations. In order to really know that you know material, say it, draw it, or teach it. Do not merely reread or look over something several times. A deeper, more active approach using the following techniques will bring you better results.

3. **Select appropriate resources:** Throughout medical school and as a physician, you will be bombarded with a variety of study materials. You will need to make decisions as to which materials are right for you. Ask the following questions.

   • What is my purpose in studying this material? Am I trying to get an overview? Am I searching for clarification or for a better explanation? Am I looking for an example?

   • What is the level of detail in this information? Do I have the background information required for understanding this material?

   • What is the format? Is it wordy? Is it written in outline form? What do the pictures, charts, and diagrams look like?

   • Do I like this resource?

Strategies for acquiring information are described in Chapter 2.

Maintenance is the second stage of learning.

Maintenance is any activity used to help you remember information, to maintain what you have acquired. How will I remember what I am learning? Effectively storing information in memory is an active, effortful process, which begins during the Acquisition stage. When you attend actively to information, it is easier to retrieve later. However, just paying attention to something, unless it is something with which you are already well-acquainted, is not enough to ensure that it will be available to you at the time of an examination several days or weeks later. Other methods are necessary. One familiar technique is rehearsal, repeating what you want to remember again and again. Although this technique may work for remembering some simple things (e.g., grocery lists), it is not an efficient strategy for handling the volume and complexity of medical school material. Other more effective strategies include:

1. **Elaboration** - linking new information with what you already know and making new information meaningful

2. **Reorganization** - grouping related pieces of information into meaningful units

3. **Cumulative review** - reviewing on a regular basis rather than cramming

4. **Mnemonics** - using specific memory techniques or tricks

Strategies for maintaining information are described in Chapter 3.

Proficiency is the third stage of learning.

Proficiency is productively using the information you have learned. In medical school, proficiency is often measured by test performance. Examinations will be important to you throughout your years in medical school, medical residency, and when you are practicing medicine, as specialty recertification is often required. Performance on examinations can be improved by taking a conscious and active role in implementing effective test-taking techniques in addition to good learning strategies. The strategies for reaching proficiency are described in Chapter 4.

Time Management

Since there is always more to do than there is time to do it in medical school, effective time management is of paramount importance, as illustrated in **Figure 1.5**. When you plan and manage your time well, and implement effective and efficient strategies for study, you will gain more confidence with the material and your feelings of stress and anxiety will be reduced.

There are several tricks to good time management in medical school.

Figure 1.5

Plan and Set Priorities

1. **Write down all the things you need to do each week.** This list should include studying, family activities, household chores, and leisure activities such as the television shows you simply cannot miss.

2. **Arrange your tasks according to importance and urgency.** One student's list might look like this:

Top priority ("I must get to these.")
- preview for Biochemistry lecture
- study Microscopic Anatomy: learn muscle tissues (examination Monday)
- group study, Gross Anatomy laboratory: thorax
- go to bank, buy dog food

Middle priority ("I'd like to get to these if at all possible.")
- catch up on Anatomy reading (innervations of organs/thorax)
- do computer questions for Microscopic Anatomy

Low priority ("I will get to these if I have time.")
- rewrite messy Biochemistry notes
- clean room
- watch ER
- buy card for friend's birthday next week
- investigate problem with car radio

3. **Develop effective and realistic deadlines.** Break larger tasks into smaller ones. It is unlikely that you will be able to memorize 50 Microscopic Anatomy slides in one sitting the day before the examination. You are more likely to accomplish this goal if you plan to do this over several study periods.

4. **Make decisions based on your own needs.** Avoid getting involved in everything everyone else does. For example, suppose you are preparing for a Biochemistry examination and have studied one topic, glycolysis, thoroughly. You are now beginning to study another topic, gluconeogenesis, when your friend asks if you want to meet with a study group to go over glycolysis. You know a review at this time might be useful. But if you go, when will you learn gluconeogenesis? It is always necessary to set priorities based on your own needs.

Schedule

1. **Plan schedules by using calendars or appointment books.** Plan by the month, by the week, and by the day. Use a daily schedule template like the one shown in **Figure 1.6**.

2. **Create your schedules in pencil** (not pen) as they are always subject to change.

3. **Schedule the most demanding tasks during the periods of your highest energy.** Do you do better in the early morning or are you a night owl?

4. **Incorporate breaks (free time) into your schedule.** This is a crucial step for medical school success. When a study schedule fails, it is usually because students have set brutal schedules that they cannot possibly maintain. Always leave time in your schedule to allow for some flexibility. Then if something happens unexpectedly or takes longer than expected, you will be able to move something into a free space. For example, if your car breaks down and you must have it fixed, a spot should be available to make up the study time that you missed. Breaks can also provide an energy boost to study more efficiently. Use breaks productively. For example, use a trip to the supermarket to take a break from studying.

Time	Sunday	Monday	Tuesday	Wednesday	Thursday	Friday	Saturday
7:30							
8:30							
9:30							
10:30							
11:30							
12:30							
1:30							
2:30							
3:30							
4:30							
5:30							
6:30							
7:30							
8:30							
9:30							
10:30							
11:30							

Figure 1.6

Eliminate Time-Wasting Activities

1. **Do not procrastinate.** Sometimes just getting started is the hardest part. Try setting a very small goal (e.g., filling in a chart for *Staphylococcus aureus*) in a small time span (e.g., 1 hour) just to get you moving. Often this can help you ease into a more intensive study session.

2. **Maintain concentration.** It makes good sense to use the time you have scheduled for study to study. However, if you find you are thinking of other things when you are supposed to be studying, you are actually wasting time. Monitor your attention and concentration at frequent intervals. If you are losing concentration, ask yourself why you cannot focus: Am I tired? Am I hungry? Am I sick of sitting at this desk? Am I worried about someone and need to make a phone call? Am I having difficulty understanding this material, and do I need to find an additional resource? Am I ready for a break? Listen to yourself, address your needs as soon as possible, and then return to more productive studying. However, if problems with concentration are frequent and persistent, it may be wise to consult with counselors who are experts in helping you learn strategies to relax and concentrate more effectively.

3. **Avoid *unscheduled* leisure activities.** Say no to questions such as, "Do you want to go to the movies?" or "Do you want to play a game of pool?" These activities can take place during planned break times.

4. **Avoid spending too much time on the telephone or in front of the TV.** Use an answering machine to screen telephone calls. Set time limits for calls and TV viewing and schedule these into your plan.

5. **Try to delegate tasks to others that are not essential to do yourself.** This could include anything from grocery shopping to taking the cat to the veterinarian.

Take a look at the sample first year medical student schedule in **Figure 1.7**. Note that initially, specific class hours are scheduled. Goals for each study block are specific and the time spent on courses is balanced. For example, it is better not to study just one subject a night, unless there is an examination the next day! Study breaks separate class time and independent study. A time slot for group study is included. Time is allotted for life-maintenance activities (laundry, meals) and leisure activities. Finally, there is some open time left in the schedule (e.g., Friday evening) in case something does not get completed.

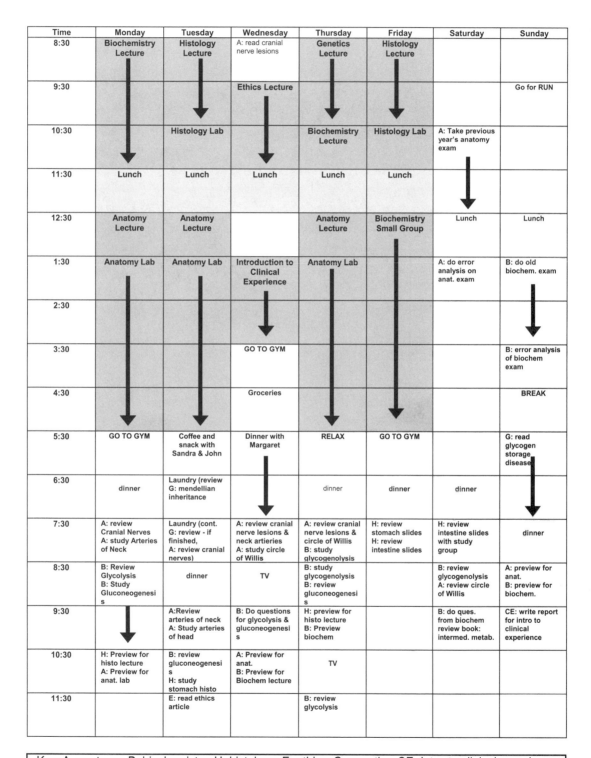

Time	Monday	Tuesday	Wednesday	Thursday	Friday	Saturday	Sunday
8:30	Biochemistry Lecture	Histology Lecture	A: read cranial nerve lesions	Genetics Lecture	Histology Lecture		
9:30			Ethics Lecture				Go for RUN
10:30		Histology Lab		Biochemistry Lecture	Histology Lab	A: Take previous year's anatomy exam	
11:30	Lunch	Lunch	Lunch	Lunch	Lunch		
12:30	Anatomy Lecture	Anatomy Lecture		Anatomy Lecture	Biochemistry Small Group	Lunch	Lunch
1:30	Anatomy Lab	Anatomy Lab	Introduction to Clinical Experience	Anatomy Lab		A: do error analysis on anat. exam	B: do old biochem. exam
2:30							
3:30			GO TO GYM				B: error analysis of biochem exam
4:30			Groceries				BREAK
5:30	GO TO GYM	Coffee and snack with Sandra & John	Dinner with Margaret	RELAX	GO TO GYM		G: read glycogen storage disease
6:30	dinner	Laundry (review G: mendellian inheritance		dinner	dinner	dinner	
7:30	A: review Cranial Nerves A: study Arteries of Neck	Laundry (cont. G: review - if finished, A: review cranial nerves)	A: review cranial lesions & neck artieries A: study circle of Willis	A: review cranial nerve lesions & circle of Willis B: study glycogenolysis	H: review stomach slides H: review intestine slides	H: review intestine slides with study group	dinner
8:30	B: Review Glycolysis B: Study Gluconeogenesis	dinner	TV	B: study glycogenolysis B: review gluconeogenesis		B: review glycogenolysis A: review circle of Willis	A: preview for anat. B: preview for biochem.
9:30		A:Review arteries of neck A: Study arteries of head	B: Do questions for glycolysis & gluconeogenesis	H: preview for histo lecture B: Preview biochem		B: do ques. from biochem review book: intermed. metab.	CE: write report for intro to clinical experience
10:30	H: Preview for histo lecture A: Preview for anat. lab	B: review gluconeogenesis H: study stomach histo	A: Preview for anat. B: Preview for Biochem lecture	TV			
11:30		E: read ethics article		B: review glycolysis			

Key: A=anatomy; B=biochemistry; H=histology; E=ethics; G=genetics; CE=Intro. to clinical experience

Figure 1.7

Notes

CHAPTER 2

ACQUISITION

Acquisition is the first stage of learning and involves the development of good understanding. In medical school, you will be acquiring information primarily from lectures, laboratories, and books. The strategies you use to acquire information have important implications for what you will later remember. Imagine trying to learn and remember the following:

The procedure is actually quite simple. First you arrange items into different groups. Of course one pile may be sufficient depending on how much there is to do. If you have to go somewhere else due to lack of facilities that is the next step; otherwise, you are pretty well set. It is important not to overdo things. That is, it is better to do too few things at once than too many. In the short run this may not seem important but complications can easily arise. A mistake can be expensive as well. At first, the whole procedure will seem complicated. Soon, however, it will become just another facet of life. It is difficult to foresee any end to the necessity for this task in the immediate future, but then, one can never tell. After the procedure is completed one arranges the materials into different groups again. Then they can be put into their appropriate places. Eventually they will be used once more and the whole cycle will then have to be repeated. However, that is part of life.

From: Bransford, J.D. & Johnson, M.K. (1972) Contextual prerequisites for understanding. Journal of Verbal Learning and Verbal Behavior, 11, p. 722. Reprinted by permission of Academic Press.

Most people find this passage difficult to comprehend and recall. How could this be improved? Your ability to remember the material would be greatly enhanced if you knew prior to reading that the passage was about *doing the laundry*. Read it over again and see how much more sense it makes. Making a connection to information you already know helps make new material more meaningful and, ultimately, more memorable. When acquiring new information, it is therefore important to stop and recall what relevant information you already know. For example, if you are about to study oxygen delivery to the tissues, you should first recall the structure and function of hemoglobin. These links will make learning new material proceed more smoothly.

Previewing

During acquisition, the most important objective is to set up a framework to enable you to add details in a meaningful way and to help you retrieve information. Specific goals for previewing include: obtaining an **overview**, becoming familiar with **vocabulary and main concepts** of the topic you are about to learn, and beginning to **generate questions** about new material. You should preview before you read a chapter, attend a lecture, or read a handout.

The Steps for Previewing

The following general steps for previewing are useful with all types of resources including handouts, class notes, textbooks, and review books.

1. **Begin by asking questions.** What do I already know about this topic or a related topic? What makes this information important? What characteristics of this organism/concept/disease make it different from others I have learned so far?

2. **Read the learning objectives first.** These objectives can be a useful guide for determining what you ultimately need to learn about the topic.

3. **Read the general summary.** This overview captures the main ideas without all the details.

4. **Read major headings.** Major headings will give you a sense of the level of detail that will be presented. Be certain to read words or concepts that appear in bold print.

5. **Look at figures, graphs, and pictures.** A picture can be worth a thousand words and can therefore illustrate a main idea concisely.

6. **Generate questions to help guide and focus your learning.** Subsequent reading can then involve searching for needed details.

Resources for Previewing

1. **Previewing Using a Review Book.** Many students find this a very effective way to preview for a lecture or before reading a text because

major concepts are presented in a succinct and logical manner and main ideas are highlighted. For example, material might be presented in an outline format, thus helping you understand the hierarchical arrangement of the material.

2. **Previewing Using a Textbook.** Although more detailed than review books, texts can be used effectively for previewing because many provide learning objectives, end-of-chapter summaries, and questions.

3. **Previewing Using a Class Handout.** Handouts usually present the information that the teacher feels is most important for a topic, often in a sequence closely resembling the structure of the lecture. Previewing using a handout can help prepare you for what the teacher will discuss, but may not necessarily be the best source for providing the big picture or framework because handouts may sometimes 1) assume that you already have some understanding of the topic (which may not be true), 2) present details that are actually less important than some of the ideas missing from the handout, and 3) be poorly organized.

4. **Previewing Using Old Scribe Notes.** Some medical schools have a scribe service (a note-taking service for lectures) which makes it possible for students to purchase the scribe notes of the previous year's lectures. If the same teacher is lecturing, it is very likely that the lecture will not have changed much from the year before. While scribe notes can be a good way to preview for a lecture, they can be problematic. First, the expertise of the student scribe will determine the quality of the information you are getting. (It is not uncommon to find glaring errors in a scribe note.) Second, scribes often rearrange the lecture to make it follow their own conceptualization of the information. This can mean that the notes no longer resemble the sequence of ideas the teacher will present. Third, many scribes may not have previewed the material themselves before they scribe a lecture and their presentation of the information can be haphazard and/or poorly explained. Using scribe notes to preview can be time-saving, but like handouts, they may not provide the best conceptual framework for the material.

5. **Previewing Using an Atlas.** In Gross and Microscopic Anatomy, it is necessary to assimilate visual information. Therefore, an atlas becomes a primary information source. The overall goal of previewing this type of information is to get a rough sketch of a detailed structure or region down first. Start by browsing the figures, noting the general placement of

structures and their relation to surrounding or other similar structures (e.g., differences between various types of epithelium, differences in orientation of muscles of the abdominal wall, etc.). Second, look at a simplified sketch of a detailed structure if available. Third, keep a review book or textbook on hand. Following along with a chart or outline while scanning pictures can be very helpful.

The amount of time you spend previewing will depend on the difficulty of the material, its importance, and the amount of time you have. (Always keep in mind the time-driven nature of medical school.) Therefore, previewing might take 10 minutes or 45 minutes. The idea is not to learn it all but to focus on primary components of the material. You will find that even if you have previewed material only for a very short time it will be more helpful than if you had not done so at all.

How to Get the Most Out of Lectures

What to Do Before a Lecture.

It is useful to prepare in advance. Preview and generate a list of questions that you want answered in the lecture. Knowing what to expect will often help you to maintain attention.

What to Do During a Lecture

Maintain attention. When you are in class, it is crucial to maintain attention. Going to class and not paying attention wastes precious learning time. Try to determine why you are having difficulty attending. Are you tired or hungry? You can help yourself maintain attention by doing the following:

1. Arrive on time. It is more difficult to follow a lecture if you come in the middle.

2. Sit in the front of the room.

3. Focus on your list of questions generated during previewing. Seeking answers will help you stay awake as well as enhance learning.

4. Take a break. If you can do so without distracting the lecturer and disturbing your colleagues, leave the room or go stand in the back of the lecture hall for a few minutes to get rejuvenated.

Distinguish which ideas are most important and likely to be tested. When the teacher spends more time on, or repeats, or shows illustrations or examples of a topic, focus on this topic. The teacher is telling you this is important. Learn it.

Take notes. Note-taking can help you pay attention, as well as serve to create essential review materials.

Note-taking during lecture

What is the most effective way to take notes during lecture? Some students try to record every word the teacher says while others do not take notes at all. Overall, it is generally more effective to take some notes than none at all. This process involves being selective about what you record because it is not useful to spend time writing information without understanding what is being said. Some pros and cons of common note-taking strategies are described (with examples) below. These should help guide your decision as to which method will work best for you.

Taking All Your Own Notes

Most students are taught to take their own notes in grammar school and high school. The student decides what is important to write down, often aided by cues from the teacher.

Pros and Cons of Taking All Your Own Notes

PROS	CONS
• You have a record of the lecture in your own words and in your own style.	• Most teachers in medical school go too fast for students to write down everything that is important. Consequently, students often miss important information because they are too busy writing.

Recommendations for Taking Your Own Notes:

- Write down only what you do not already know.

- Previewing will help you determine what material is essential to record.

Annotating

When handouts are available, many students like to follow along in class and add information as the teacher addresses each topic. The teacher may add explanations and examples that will help jog your memory when you review the material. Annotating the handout is usually an efficient method of note-taking in lectures. You do not have to organize the material on the spot. Your annotations will give you a reference point for what the teacher is saying, and will enable you to clarify information.

Instructors often deliver more or less the same lecture on a specific topic for many years, and the lecture format and content are not likely to change much over time. Therefore, it is useful to highlight the things that the lecturer emphasizes, and add any new material in the margins of the handout. **Figure 2.1** is an example of an annotated handout on cells of the immune system.

Pros and Cons of Annotating Handouts

PROS	CONS
• The entire lecture is often printed right in front of you, word for word. • It does not require that you take down everything that was said during the lecture, allowing you to spend more time paying attention to meaning. • Slides shown in class are often included as figures.	• Handouts can be poorly organized. • There may not be much space for writing. • Since handouts are often given at the start of the class, predicting how much you may need to write is difficult. • If the lecture has changed, you may spend too much time searching for the information.

Recommendations for Annotating:

- Use the back of the page or add blank pages if more room is needed.

- Previewing will help give you a sense of how much writing you will need to do during lecture.

CELLS OF THE IMMUNE SYSTEM

cell mediated vs. humoral T vs. B

Immunity can be broken down into two basic categories - cell-mediated immunity and humoral (antibody-mediated) immunity. The roles of the various immune cells are varied; however, there is a great deal of overlap between them. Some generalizations can be noted: they are all activated in one way or another and they all interact with other immune cells. There are also numerous differences: they each respond to different things (although many respond to similar things as well), they each have specific cell surface markers that identify them as unique, and so forth. The major immune cells are described below.

function as APCs, phagocytose, form monocytes

Macrophages are the main antigen presenting cells of the immune system. They phagocytose incoming bacteria and present them to helper T-cells in association with major histocompatibility (MHC) antigen class II. These cells are derived from the monocyte line.

all have CD3-cytotoxic: CD8 & MHC I-helper: CD4 & MHC II

T-cells universally express CD3. They can be divided into two subclasses based on their functions, their cell-surface markers, and the antigen classes with which they react. The cytotoxic T-cells express CD8 and interact with the MHC antigen class I. The helper T-cell population express CD4 and interact with MHC antigen class II.

Figure 2.1

What to Do After a Lecture

1. **Review as soon as possible.** You are more likely to remember what has been said and what you did not understand if you review soon after a lecture. Waiting a few days or longer before reviewing will make it much more difficult to recall important details. Determine what material is clear and what needs clarification. Begin to fill in the gaps by reading a textbook, going to speak to the lecturer, or getting help from a peer.

2. **Summarize/restate/rephrase the information in your own words.** This helps to make the information more meaningful and assures understanding.

3. **Reformat the information** in a way that is useful for studying. You may find that there are pieces of information that belong together but that are not presented together during the lecture. For example, an instructor may return to a topic several times, making a few points each time. In the notes you reformat, put all the information pertaining to a topic into a single place.

Using Your Textbook Effectively

Most medical students find that instead of reading their textbook assignments cover to cover as they probably did in college, they often read only small sections of the text to clarify information presented in lecture. Focused reading, i.e., reading only pertinent small sections of the text to clarify information, is common. In other situations (if a student has not attended a lecture, does not have a handout for the material, or has not been able to make adequate sense of most of what was presented in a lecture), reading more of the textbook is necessary. For efficiency, it is best to choose one definitive primary source from among the suggested, required, and recommended texts. In many cases, good understanding of material comes from getting the story from one place. Additional texts should be used only when your primary choice of text does not provide sufficient detail or does not make the information clear.

How to Approach Science Texts

1. **Preview** and look to see how the information is organized.

2. **Pay attention to the format**, such as main headings, subheadings, color coding, diagrams, charts, photographs, and general physical arrangement.

3. **Read for a purpose** and adjust your rate to that purpose. **Develop questions** in advance and then find the answers. This is the hallmark of active learning. At first your questions may be general, e.g., What are the important elements of bacterial cell structure? These should develop into more specific compare-and-contrast questions as you learn the material, e.g., What makes the Gram-positive cell wall different from the Gram-negative cell wall?

4. **Identify unfamiliar vocabulary.** If the meaning of a word is essential in order to make sense of what you are reading, look it up immediately. Have medical and nonmedical dictionaries handy.

5. **Look for relationships.** Do not read text as just a collection of facts. Consider how new information fits with information presented previously.

6. **Make sure you understand the main ideas.** Many students get lost in the details and miss the big picture. This attention to the details at the expense of the general ideas makes it difficult to apply the information to novel situations and scenarios that appear on tests.

7. **Assess your comprehension** at frequent intervals. **Summarize** after studying a meaningful chunk of information. **Restate** things in your own words. Your goal should be to rephrase the information accurately, in a way that makes sense to you.

8. **Monitor your concentration** at frequent intervals. Stay alert. Avoid reading the text as if it were a novel.

9. **Assess your need for additional resources.** These resources may take the form of teachers, peers, dictionaries, or other books. Is the textbook answering all of your questions? Or is it insufficient in some way (e.g., lacking clarity or detail)?

10. **Develop a note-taking system.** How will you remember without rereading the text? Decide on a format and how much detail you will include. Note-taking is discussed further below.

Note-taking from a textbook

Your overall goal when taking notes should be to condense all the information for a given topic into one source to review. This process may entail adding some details from the text into an already fairly complete handout or set of scribe notes. At other times, it may mean taking notes from the text and then adding material from other sources. It is much more efficient to have one definitive source from which to review information than to try to use several sources. *Integrate information as much as possible and avoid redundancy.*

1. **Highlighting:** Students often use a highlighter to emphasize important ideas. Highlighting becomes popular in college, when students often own their books for the first time. However, many students over-highlight. It is common to look at a medical student's books and see entire pages of text highlighted without a break! This obviously defeats the purpose. Highlighting can be very passive, as students may take a *this-looks-important-I'll-study-it-later* approach. Highlighting must be done actively to distinguish important information from irrelevant details and to sort what you know from what you still need to learn.

Pros and Cons of Highlighting

PROS	CONS
• It can help you focus on important points. • It takes less time than outlining.	• Things that are not highlighted may be completely ignored, and important details may be missed. • Highlighting does not allow you to reorganize information. • It is hard to control the urge to highlight everything (highlighting can become automatic and passive).

Recommendations for Highlighting:

• Avoid the compulsion to highlight everything.

• Only highlight information that you do not already know.

• Try to highlight key words or sentences instead of long passages. This strategy will help you to focus when you review. You can always choose to read more than what is highlighted.

2. **Annotating:** Writing in the textbook, and jotting in the margins and around the figures, can help clarify and consolidate information. This is especially helpful for visual information because material relating to a figure is consolidated along with the picture, providing an excellent source for review. **Figure 2.2** is an example of an annotated picture.

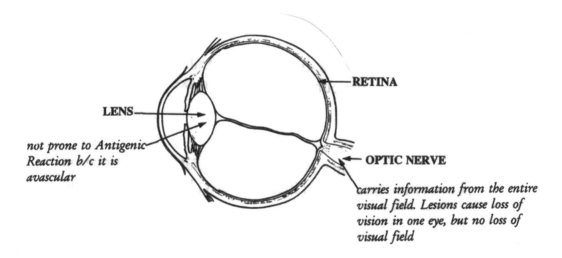

Figure 2.2

Pros and Cons of Annotating

PROS	CONS
• The pictures become focal points for information and good sources for review. • Annotating is faster than outlining and more active than highlighting.	• There may not be enough room to annotate. • Organization can become a problem if there is too much information to include.

Recommendation for Annotating:

- Photocopy figures from books. Enlarge these or blank out surrounding text to make room for annotation.

3. **Outlining**: Outlining is especially useful for information that needs to be arranged hierarchically, but the method can be overused.

Pros and Cons of Outlining

PROS	CONS
• It is a familiar method. • Hierarchical organization is easy to follow and is good for studying levels of detail.	• Often outlining is done mechanically. • Information may not lend itself to outline format. • Outlining does not highlight key relationships, such as comparisons. • Outlining may take too much time.

Recommendations for Outlining:

- Use the book divisions for section headings of your outline.

- Only write down information that you do not already know.

- Tag your notes to indicate where important graphs, pictures, and tables are found in the book. You can then refer to these later, and/or photocopy and attach to your notes.

4. **Other Forms of Note-taking:** The types of note-taking methods described are often intermediate steps in learning. That is, students often take notes and then condense them to create materials to review for examinations. However, many students skip the note-taking methods described in this chapter and are able to create better review formats early on. These formats are addressed in Chapter 3.

Points to Remember About Note-taking:

- Determine your note-taking method and the amount of detail you need to include according to your stage in the learning process. For example, are you clarifying information at the acquisition stage, developing review materials, or writing key words to reach proficiency?

- Avoid writing down material you already know. Your job is not to write an entire review book for someone else!

- Self-monitor: Constantly re-evaluate your note-taking approach by asking, Is it efficient? Is it effective? Is it the best way to consolidate this information?

Notes

CHAPTER 3

MAINTENANCE

Maintenance, or keeping information in memory, takes work. We do not retain much information without making a conscious effort to do so. Naturally, certain information is easily retained in memory if used frequently. For example, if you moved to a new city, at first you would need to make a deliberate effort to recall the route from work to home. However, as you took this route regularly you wouldn't really need to think about how to get home because this becomes automatic. Unfortunately, most of what you will need to learn in medical school takes work.

Think back to the penny example described in Chapter 1. An important reason that people find it difficult to recognize or draw the face of a penny accurately has to do with the way the information was processed during acquisition. For most people (except perhaps those who design or collect coins), the details on the face of a penny are not very important. When information is not relevant we often ignore it, and consequently, we have difficulty when we try to recall it. This difficulty can occur even though we may have seen the information many times. The difficulty encountered when trying to remember such familiar information surprises people because familiarity with something suggests that we should know it. The penny example illustrates three essential points:

First, *maintaining information in memory actually begins during acquisition*. If you knew you would be asked to draw the penny, you would have directed your attention to more of the details: which way Lincoln is facing, the placement of the word liberty, the date, etc. Actively attending to information helps make that information easier to retrieve later. You can remember course material more effectively by staying alert during acquisition. Ask yourself questions about the material and focus on finding specific answers to your questions.

Second, *it is most effective to try to remember something in a form that matches the way you will be tested*. If you knew you would be asked to draw a penny you would prepare for the test effectively by studying and then drawing the penny from memory. Therefore, for medical school examinations, it is important to know what proficiency demands will be expected of you so that you can study and test your knowledge in the most directly analogous way. For example, if you need to know the relative location of structures in Gross Anatomy, you will want to note the relationships between structures and then try to draw those structures, showing the relationships, from memory.

Third, *familiarity with material should not be used as the gauge by which to measure knowledge.* Just because you have seen, heard, or read something (even several times) does not ensure that you really know that material. Do not evaluate your level of knowledge by depending on feelings of knowing. Test yourself to determine whether you have actually committed the material to memory. A detailed description of self-assessment will be described in Chapter 4.

Memory Strategies...How to Hang on to Information

Rehearsal

Rehearsal means repeating what you want to remember over and over again. Rote memorization is a familiar technique used, for example, to remember a phone number just before dialing. This strategy works well for holding on to some information in short-term memory, but it is not an effective strategy for remembering the volume and complexity of medical school material, which needs to be remembered over the long-term. Information remembered via rote memorization is quickly forgotten. Reviewing can help you remember, but reviewing and re-reviewing all of the information you will need to master for medical school tests is not feasible. Rehearsal alone is therefore not an effective memory strategy.

Creating Meaning

Suppose you need to remember the phone number for a physician referral service: 1-800-DOCTORS. You are likely to find this number easy to remember because the pattern is meaningful. There are four ways to make information more meaningful.

1. **Make use of prior knowledge**. Take a look at **Figure 3.1**, the signs used to classify the severity of acute pancreatitis.

Ransom's Prognostic Criteria for Acute Pancreatitis

Present on admission:

Age>55 years
White blood cell count>16,000/µL
Blood glucose>200 mg/dL
Serum LDH>350 IU/L
SGOT (AST)>250 IU/dL

Developing during first 48 h:

Hematocrit fall>10%
BUN increase>8 mg/dL
Serum Ca^{+2}<8 mg/dL
Arterial PO_2<60 mmHg

Morbidity and mortality rates correlate with the number of criteria present:
0-2 = 2% mortality; 3-4 = 15% mortality; 5-6 = 40% mortality;
7-8 = 10% mortality.

Figure 3.1

From: Schwartz, Seymour I., M.D. (1993) **Principles of Surgery - Companion Handbook**, 6th edition, p. 502. Reprinted by permission of McGraw-Hill.

Students who attempt to learn this material as separate details through rote memorization run into difficulties. The information can be learned and remembered better by conceptualizing the material in a framework that you *understand* first, before trying to learn the details. Knowledge about the normal state of the pancreas will enable you to make better sense of this information. For example, understanding the role of the pancreas in producing insulin and regulating blood sugar enables you to predict what may occur in pancrea*titis*, i.e., when the pancreas is inflamed. One would expect the white blood cell count and blood glucose levels to be abnormal because the organ is in an abnormal state. The values in the chart reflect this assumption by indicating that white blood cell and glucose levels are high. Likewise, recalling the functional relationship between the liver and pancreas will enable you to make better sense of the way that this disorder affects liver enzymes. Giving details meaning can help you remember them much more effectively.

2. **Elaborate.** Elaboration, or expanding upon information beyond what is presented, is another method for making material more memorable. Elaboration involves relying on prior knowledge and processing new material with deeper understanding. This can be effectively accomplished by creating analogies (e.g., This reminds me of...) or by making predictions about material (e.g., I think this would happen if ...). For example, when studying respiratory physiology, you will learn the definition of shunt: when blood that normally would be conveyed to the lungs for oxygenation is instead sent back into the systemic circulation or sent to a portion of the lung where oxygenation cannot occur. It is useful to try to predict what will happen if a shunt is present. For example, you might ask the questions: Will there be cyanosis? Will the oxygen saturation of the blood go up or down? Will there be a redirection of blood to areas of good ventilation? How can I measure the amount of shunt a patient has?

3. **Integrate information.** In medical school material is often presented in a segmented way where topics appear to be detached from one another. For example, in Biochemistry, topics may appear on a syllabus like this:

   I.   Glycolysis
   II. Gluconeogenesis
   III. The Krebs Cycle
   IV. Oxidative Phosphorylation

In your lectures and even in textbooks, little effort may be made to link these topics together as different branches of intermediate metabolism. Therefore, students often study these topics in isolation by trying to memorize each pathway, the enzymes involved, and the regulatory steps, as if each topic were unrelated to the others. However, examination questions require an understanding of how different pathways are integrated. The information needs to be synthesized in order to do well on examinations. It is best to think about how an enzyme deficiency in one cycle affects the functioning of other cycles and other parts of the system. It is essential to integrate various pieces of related information to make the connections that are necessary for effective learning.

4. **Use clinical examples.** Make basic science information more interesting and memorable by using clinical examples. Students can find learning basic science material as detached from the real tasks of being a competent doctor. It is helpful to give what you are learning a sense of relevance. For example, rather than simply trying to memorize the biochemical cycles of intermediate metabolism, you should consider various metabolic disorders,

how patients with such disorders may look, and think through why a particular enzyme deficiency leads to the observed symptoms. Or when learning the innervation of the lower limb in Gross Anatomy, consider what symptoms a lesion to each of the nerves would produce. If you can associate these symptoms with the causes of them, you will enhance your ability to remember which muscles are innervated by which nerves. Using clinical examples can help you maintain interest and remain attentive and focused.

Information That Is Organized Will Be More Easily Remembered

Imagine having to remember the following list of letters:

M T V C I A N B C F A A

Learning this list by rehearsing it would be time-consuming and inefficient. Remembering the same list of letters as MTV, CIA, NBC, FAA is easier because the letters are now organized in a meaningful way. Although both lists contain 12 letters, the second list contains 4 memorable chunks, thereby reducing memory load. If the list is changed again by organizing the four groups into two categories, TV Stations and Government Agencies, memory load is reduced even further. You now need to remember only two categories to recall the 12 original letters. Organizing information will allow you to recall it in a more efficient manner, and information that is meaningfully organized will be more memorable.

Storing information in memory is analogous to storing information in a file cabinet. If you toss files into a cabinet haphazardly, you are likely to have difficulty retrieving a particular file. Locating the file might take you some time, the job would be frustrating, and perhaps the file might appear to be lost. Similarly, if you toss information into your head without paying attention to where you are placing it in your memory, the information will be difficult to retrieve later on. Locating it may become frustrating or impossible. Storing the information you are learning efficiently, in an organized fashion (similar to categorizing folders in a file cabinet), will enable you to retrieve it more quickly and accurately, an essential component for building confidence on examinations.

Information presented in your textbooks, lectures, and handouts may not be presented in an organized, accessible, concise format. Information about a given topic may be scattered on several pages throughout one or more chapters, or topics may not be presented in a useful sequence. Reorganizing information through note-taking is an effective way to consolidate information. For example, the chart in **Figure 3.2** summarizes where the cranial nerves exit the skull. The information is organized by exit locations: four nerves exit the superior orbital fissure, three nerves exit the jugular foramen, etc. This one table concisely summarizes information found on several pages of a textbook and can provide a convenient source for review. Such summaries, which can also be found in textbooks and review books, consolidate details that can become buried within text.

It is useful to identify a format for consolidating information during previewing when you are becoming familiar with the overall nature of the material and getting the big picture. For example, if you decide the material, such as embryonic development, is best learned sequentially, ordered lists or flow charts as shown in **Figure 3.3** will be useful. If comparisons, such as differentiating features of immune cells, are involved, charts will be more useful. (**Figure 3.4**)

Cranial Nerve Exits	
Nerve	**Cranial Exit**
I: Olfactory	Cribriform foramina
II: Optic	Optic canal
III: Oculomotor	Superior orbital fissure
IV: Trochlear	Superior orbital fissure
V: Trigeminal	Superior orbital fissure; foramen rotundum; foramen ovale
VI: Abducens	Superior orbital fissure
VII: Facial	Stylomastoid foramen
VIII: Vestibulocochlear	Does not leave skull
IX: Glossopharyngeal	Jugular foramen
X: Vagus	Jugular foramen
XI: Accessory	Jugular foramen
XII: Hypoglossal	Hypoglossal canal

Figure 3.2

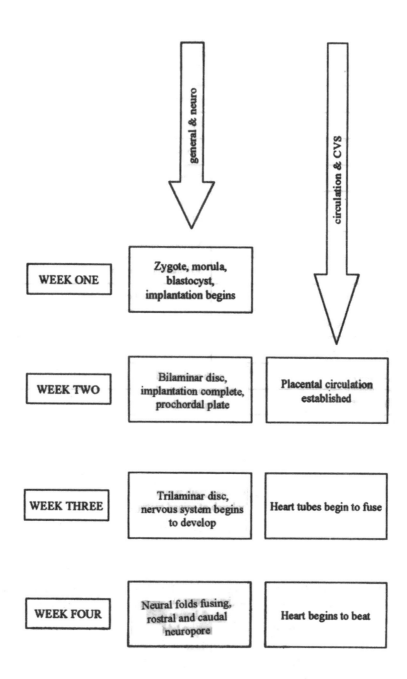

Figure 3.3

CELL TYPE	SURFACE MOLECULES	RESPONDS TO/DOES

Helper T-cells	• CD4
	• TCR
	• IL-2R
	• CD3
		• Antigen-presenting cells: MHC class II
		• Regulatory functions:
		  • activate B-cells via IL-4 & IL-5
		  • make IL-2
		  • make gamma interferon
		• Effector function:
		  • mediate delayed hypersensitivity

Cytotoxic T-cells	• CD8 • TCR • IL-2R • CD3	• Virus infected cells: MHC class I • Effector functions: • kill virus-infected cells, tumor cells, allografts
B-cells	• IgM	• Antigen binds IgM on surface (also responds to helper T-cells which activate B-cells) • Make antibodies

Figure 3.4

Mnemonics

You are probably very familiar with mnemonics. You may have learned to spell Mississippi by singing the letters, you may have learned the sentence "**E**very **G**ood **B**oy **D**oes **F**ine" to remember the lines of the staff when learning to read music, or you may have used ROY-G-BIV to recall the colors in the spectrum (**R**ed, **O**range, **Y**ellow, **G**reen, **B**lue, **I**ndigo, **V**iolet.) Mnemonics rely on associations, but unlike elaborative processing, most mnemonics do not associate information in an intrinsically meaningful way. They do not help to explain anything about the information you are trying to remember. Consequently, these memory strategies have limited utility in medical school, and should be used only as a last resort. There are several kinds of mnemonics.

The peg-word mnemonic

This can be used to recall a list of items, such as the list of cranial nerves. The first step would be to learn a simple rhyme (one is a bun, two is a shoe, three is a tree, etc.). The next step would be to associate each of the new words you want to remember with the rhyming words on the list. The olfactory nerve (cranial nerve I), therefore, becomes associated with "one is a bun." To remember this, you might create a visual image of a large nose (since olfactory deals with smell) sitting on top of a bun. The optic nerve (cranial nerve II) then becomes associated with "two is a shoe." You might make an image of a large eyeball sitting inside a shoe. While this technique is effective for helping to remember names of items in sequence, it should be apparent that you do not actually *learn* anything meaningful about the information by using this strategy (e.g., the function of the nerves, their innervations, etc.).

Acronyms

These are commonly used mnemonics, created by taking the first letters of the words you need to remember and forming a new word. Each of the letters in the acronym should provide a trigger for making the association to each of the original items. For example, to remember the names of the viruses that cause gastroenteritis: Norwalk, rota, adeno, one student created the acronym NO ROAD GAS. (Thanks to Lawrence Janowski, M.D. for this mnemonic).

Stories, rhymes, songs, and silly sayings

These are also mnemonics. You may remember learning the alphabet song and the number of days in each month by chanting "Thirty days hath September, April, June and November..." A medical student made up this mnemonic to remember the names and order of the cranial nerves:

"**O**ooh, **O**ooh, **O**ooh, **T**o **T**ouch **A**nd **F**eel **V**ery **G**ood **V**arnish, **A**H"

O: Olfactory (CN I)
O: Optic (CN II)
O: Oculomotor (CN III)
T: Trochlear (CN IV)
T: Trigeminal (CN V)
A: Abducens (CN VI)
F: Facial (CN VII)
V: Vestibulocochlear (CN VIII)
G: Glossopharyngeal (CN IX)
V: Vagus (CN X)
A: Accessory (CN XI)
H: Hypoglossal (CN XII)

Published mnemonics (for remembering both basic and clinical science information) can be found in a number of books. But be cautious—mnemonics can become easily jumbled and forgotten and using too many will detract from your learning.

Cumulative Review and Spaced Practice

The use of cumulative review and spaced practice will help you remember more. Have you ever crammed for a test? It may have worked when you needed to memorize material for a test the next day, but it is likely that you forgot much of the material shortly thereafter. Cramming in medical school will prove especially detrimental as you prepare for cumulative examinations, for licensure examinations, and ultimately, for building the knowledge base needed in your work as a physician.

Engaging in review will enhance long-term memory. Effective medical students review material regularly by beginning each study session with a brief overview of the material covered during a previous study session. For example, an effective approach to learning the pathways and innervations of the cranial nerves would be:

Study session 1:

Study pathways and innervations of cranial nerves I, II, and III.

Study session 2:

Review nerves I, II, and III. To gain maximum benefit, sketch out these pathways from memory.
Study pathways and innervations of nerves IV, V, and VI.

Study session 3:

Review the first six nerves with less time spent reviewing I, II, and III, and more time reviewing IV, V, and VI.

Over time, perhaps by the end of a week, the student will have learned all cranial nerves. However, this material will need to be reviewed or will be quickly forgotten. So, in another week, the material should be reviewed to make sure it is retained, and this review should occur each week up until the examination. This spaced practice will help the student develop a sense of mastery and control over the information. Engaging in frequent review of small units of information at regular intervals is more productive than reviewing all of the material at one time.

CHAPTER 4

PROFICIENCY

Proficiency means learning material so that you can *utilize it effectively.* Reaching proficiency (being prepared for an examination) will depend upon how well you implement strategies during the learning stages of Acquisition and Maintenance. This chapter describes activities useful in your final preparation for examinations that will help you feel more confident and in control of the material you have studied. To reach this level of proficiency, you will need to organize time and resources, utilize active strategies for review, engage in self-assessment to guide further study, and practice effective test-taking strategies.

Organize Time and Resources

Deciding what material should be reviewed, scheduling review time, and selecting resources for review are essential elements of final preparation for examinations.

Set priorities

Because it will not be possible to review everything you have studied, you will need to decide on a hierarchy of topics for study. Select these as high priority: topics that will take the most time and effort, topics you found difficult to learn, information you had trouble recalling during previous study sessions, and material that you may not have studied at all (e.g., new information presented in lecture shortly before an examination). Set other priorities based on course emphasis. For example, if there were two lectures given on topic A and one on topic B, topic A probably will be more heavily represented on the test.

Prepare a schedule

Make it reasonable (do not plan to study all priority topics in one study block) as well as feasible (one that you can live with). Remember, you are unlikely to have time to review everything. It is better to schedule short, focused study blocks than to spend extended periods (many hours or full days) on one subject or topic. Strategies for managing time and scheduling have already been addressed in Chapter 1.

Select resources

Choose resources for review that help to compare and integrate information. Use the condensed charts, diagrams, and flow charts that you have created, supplemented, or annotated. If you need more information, return to focused text readings. Avoid the urge to read everything again as this will be impossible to accomplish.

Utilize Active Strategies for Review

Active review means testing yourself so that you are certain you know the information. Remember the penny example! It is not enough to just look over material several times and feel familiar with it to be adequately prepared for a test. You must work to *recall* information. You should not count on being able to recognize the correct answer on the test.

When beginning your review of a topic, it is useful to start by **generating** all the information you can about it first. What do you know? Write, draw, or repeat what you can from memory. Next, check your accuracy by looking at your review materials. This method will help you determine what you already know and what you still need to learn. It will help you avoid studying review materials passively as a script or narrative.

Consider group study as a way to increase active learning and review. Evaluate your knowledge by teaching others about a topic. As you present information, you will quickly realize what you know well and what you do not. Listen carefully for accuracy while other group members present material. Solicit questions and answers to clarify material and challenge your level of understanding.

Engage in Self-assessment to Guide Further Study

After studying to the point where you think you know the information, be certain to test yourself more formally (using test questions) to ensure that you are learning in a way that will lead to success on examinations. There are many resources for practice questions. The best questions will be those from actual old examinations, which may be available to you. Other sources for questions are review books and computer test banks.

It is best to utilize practice questions well before the actual examinations to identify gaps in your learning. Do not wait until you feel ready for the entire examination. Test yourself regularly during the interval between examinations. Students often set weekly goals, studying topics covered each week as if studying for a quiz, and then test themselves on these topics at the end of that week. The main objective of this method is to identify areas of weakness and to target topics for follow-up study well in advance of the actual test. As an examination approaches, the mock quizzes should include more topics so that shortly before an examination (perhaps a week prior), your quizzes include all of the topics to be covered (composite assessments). Fine tune your studying by analyzing errors, and then focus on topics you are missing. Score these assessments to monitor your progress and to help you predict the outcome of the actual examination.

Suggestions for using practice questions are as follows:

1. **Simulate the conditions of an actual examination.** Take questions in a single, timed setting. Remember, getting a question correct after spending 10 minutes on it is quite different from completing questions under stringent time constraints (1 or 2 minutes per question.) Do a set of questions rather than looking up answers to each as you proceed.

2. **If the question set is long, do every other or every third question.** This is a way to ensure that you will complete questions from many topics while reducing the amount of time that you need.

3. **Use a separate, numbered answer sheet.** This not only simulates test conditions, but it also provides a useful format for completing an error analysis (see below).

4. **Complete an error analysis.** Analyzing your errors means identifying why you got a question wrong. This will signal what changes in your study and test-taking strategies will be most beneficial, and particularly what topics need continued focus. Identifying patterns of errors will help you eliminate those that are posing the most difficulties. Use an error analysis form, such as the one included at the end of this chapter, to help you classify your mistakes.

Errors on examinations fall into three categories: content errors, errors in application of information, and errors due to ineffective test-taking strategies.

Content errors are made for several reasons:

1. **You may never have come across the information during study or you may have decided not to study some information because it did not seem to be a priority.** As you set priorities and choose topics to study, it is possible to miss some information. If such errors are relatively few, it suggests that you have usually set the right priorities and studied them in sufficient detail. However, if you frequently omit important material, it indicates that you must adjust the way you are making decisions about what to study, or that you need to make revisions to the way you are managing time.

2. **You may have learned information incorrectly.** These types of errors are less common but extremely frustrating. It is essential to catch these mistakes early in order to learn the material correctly.

3. **You may remember studying information but could not recall the specific details needed for the test question.** These errors are very frustrating because you are aware of the information, and may even be able to picture some of it in your notes or text, but you cannot recall the specifics well enough to come up with a response. These memory errors relate to ineffective maintenance strategies. Regular review of condensed materials that are organized in a meaningful format will help you retrieve information more easily at examination time.

Application Errors

These occur when you have a good grasp of basic facts but are unable to apply that knowledge to new situations. These problem-solving errors are best overcome by practicing problems as part of your study routine and challenging your understanding of the material. For example, when studying Biochemistry, you might ask, "How would the citric acid cycle be affected by a thiamine deficiency?" In Physiology, your question might be "How would the body's electrolyte balance be altered by a disorder that disrupts the functioning of the collecting tubules?" Being certain that material is learned in a meaningful way, rather than just memorizing it, will help avoid mistakes in application.

Test-taking Errors

These mechanical errors are the result of misreading or misinterpreting questions or responding impulsively to multiple choice questions, that is, jumping to an answer. The most effective way to overcome these types of errors is through careful reading and a methodical test-taking strategy.

Test-taking Strategies

1. **Pace yourself.** Determine the amount of time allowed for an examination and the number of questions you must answer. Set up checkpoints to determine whether you need to speed up or slow down. For example, if the examination allots 1 minute per question, check yourself after about 20 questions to see that you are approximately at the 20-minute mark.

2. **Read carefully for comprehension, not speed.** Underline key information. Examination questions often require reasoning and inference. Paying attention to the information given in each question is paramount. Careful reading is also the way to avoid missing cues and key words. Avoid rereading because it is inefficient.

3. **Restate the question.** To make sure you really understand what a question is asking, it is useful to stop and rephrase the information in your own words. Start thinking about pertinent information, even if you cannot immediately generate an answer.

4. **Carefully analyze each answer.** Read each of the answer choices separately and rate each option. It is best to cover all the other choices to increase your focus/concentration on each and to help remain objective. For each option, mark:

T	I am very certain that this is true.
T?	I am not certain, but I think this is true.
F?	I am not certain, but I think this is false.
F	I am very certain that this is false.
?	I have no idea.

If you end up with two answers marked similarly (T, T, or T?, T?) take another look. Assess your level of certainty about each and choose the best answer.

5. **Do test questions in sequence and mark the answer sheet after every item.** This is particularly important for examinations given under stringent time constraints because you may not have time to go back to earlier questions. If you are very uncertain about an answer choice, mark the question so that if you have time, you can go back and look at it again. Change an answer only if you are confident that your original answer is incorrect. This may happen if information in another question jogs your memory.

6. **Accept questions at face value.** Do not assume that examination questions are meant to trick or **trap you.** Some questions may seem too easy. If you prepare well for examinations, you will feel confident in your knowledge and realize that a question may be easy because you really know the material!

7. If your score on the examination is based solely on the number of correct answers obtained, answer every question even if you have no clue and are merely guessing.

FORM FOR ERROR ANALYSIS (See **Figure 4.1**)

Directions:

1. Review your examination sequentially. Write down the number of each question missed in Column A and the topic of the question in Column B. As an example: the topic of a Gross Anatomy question might be upper limb/nerve injuries or thorax/mediastinum.

2. Check the reason for each error in Columns C, D, and E. (Example: If the correct answer seems obvious it suggests you may have misread or misinterpreted the question previously and you would check Column C.)

3. Record errors on the entire examination in this way.

4. Count and record the number of questions you got wrong in each category. Identify error patterns and revise your study plan and strategies. Example: If 8 of 11 errors are due to your having studied but couldn't recall, then you need to work on implementing memorization and review techniques. If 8 of 11 errors are due to misreading of the question, then you need to work on your test-taking skills.

Figure 4.1 Form for Error Analysis

SUBJECT: _____

DATE OF EXAMINATION: _____

TOPICS COVERED: _____

A	B	C CONTENT			D APPLICATION	E TEST-TAKING	
Q #	TOPIC	Never saw	Decided not to study	Studied but learned incorrectly	Studied but could not recall	Studied and remembered basic info, but could not apply it to question	Misread/ misinterpreted	Impulsive/ over-confident
ERROR TALLY:								

Notes

PART II

STRATEGIES FOR STUDYING COURSES

CHAPTER 5

STRATEGIES FOR
STUDYING
GROSS ANATOMY

Gross Anatomy is the detailed study of the large, macroscopically visible structures of the body, including the muscles, bones, joints, blood vessels, and internal organs. You will need to know the relative locations of particular structures, their importance as structural and functional units, and the basis of the embryological development. Typically, structures must be visualized relative to other structures. You will also learn to use a vast new vocabulary because this class is usually taught early in the medical school curriculum. A key to success is to assimilate information from a variety of sources: material presented in lectures, read from your textbooks, and discovered during dissections in the laboratory.

Chapter Overview

A. Use words to guide you through the pictures since Gross Anatomy is a visual subject.

B. Learn terminology in a meaningful way. The words will often direct you.

C. Pay attention to the relative locations of structures. Focus on how each structure fits in with surrounding structures.

D. Identify an anchor point and build your knowledge around it.

E. Learn major structures in a simplified form first.

F. Draw structures from memory to see how well you know them.

G. Study the connections between regions.

H. Consolidate and organize information.

I. Review cumulatively.

J. Use Gross Anatomy laboratory time effectively.

K. Become familiar with the types of questions you will be asked.

A. Use words to guide you through the pictures since Gross Anatomy is a visual subject.

It is not useful just to read a Gross Anatomy textbook. You must make a constant correlation between written information and pictorial information. For example, if asked to learn the information below, it is essential to refer to the accompanying figure as you read. While reading the passage, look for the structures described in the diagram. (**Figure 5.1**) It is always useful to keep a medical dictionary handy to look up words you do not know.

The heart has four chambers - two atria and two ventricles. The right atrium is fed by the superior and inferior vena cava, which carry deoxygenated blood from the systemic circulation. The blood passes through the tricuspid valve into the right ventricle and leaves the right ventricle through the pulmonary valve. It then travels in the pulmonary arteries to the lungs, where it is oxygenated. The oxygenated blood travels to the left atrium via the four pulmonary veins. Blood leaves the left atrium through the mitral valve and enters the left ventricle. Blood leaves the left ventricle by passing through the aortic valve and entering the aorta.

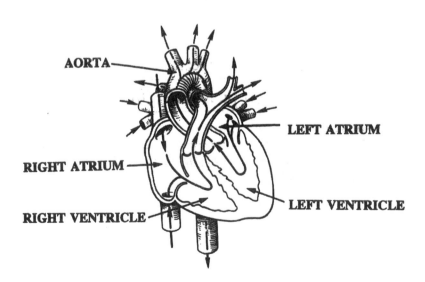

Figure 5.1

B. Learn terminology in a meaningful way. The words will often direct you.

Instead of trying to memorize the name of each structure, learn the Latin and Greek roots of the words. There are two advantages to this:

- you will be able to predict the names of other structures, and

- you will often learn that the names themselves reveal characteristics of the structure that make it easier to recall.

For example,

myo (muscle)+	cardium (heart)	Myocardium
myo (muscle)+	blast (immature cell)	Myoblast
myo (muscle)+	oma (tumor)	Myoma

Similarly,

- supra- (above): The supraduodenal artery is located above the duodenum.
- infra- (below): The infratemporal fossa is below the temple.

C. Pay attention to the relative locations of structures. Focus on how each structure relates to its surrounding structures.

Follow the path a structure takes and consciously note where it passes in relation to the other regional structures. Learn by describing structures using anatomical terms. For example, look at **Figure 5.2** and identify that the common carotid artery can be described as:

- anterior to the vagus nerve
- anterior to the superior cervical cardiac nerve

- medial to the subclavian artery (at its base)
- slightly posterolateral and deep to the thyroid gland

D.   Identify an anchor point and build knowledge around it.

When you are faced with learning many structures in a small region, identify one that is both large and relatively invariable from person to person and use it as an anchor point. The other structures in that region can then be learned by their placement in relation to that anchor point. For example, using **Figure 5.2**, the common carotid artery can be used as the anchor point for other structures in the neck. Learning the placement of the other structures is simply a matter of learning where they are in relation to the common carotid artery.

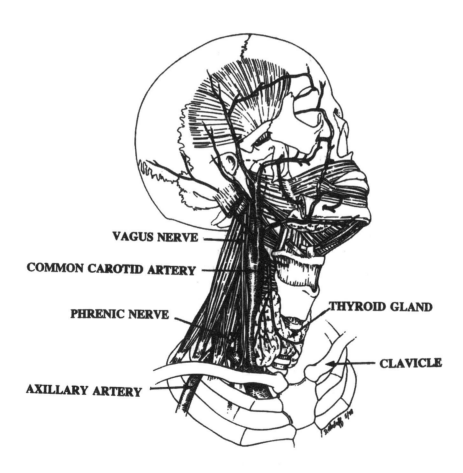

VAGUS NERVE

COMMON CAROTID ARTERY

PHRENIC NERVE

THYROID GLAND

CLAVICLE

AXILLARY ARTERY

Figure 5.2

E. Learn major structures in a simplified form first.

Begin by learning a simplified form of a complicated structure. Then move to more detailed material (ultimately, the atlas). For example, when studying the brachial plexus:

First learn a simple sketch. (**Figure 5.3**)

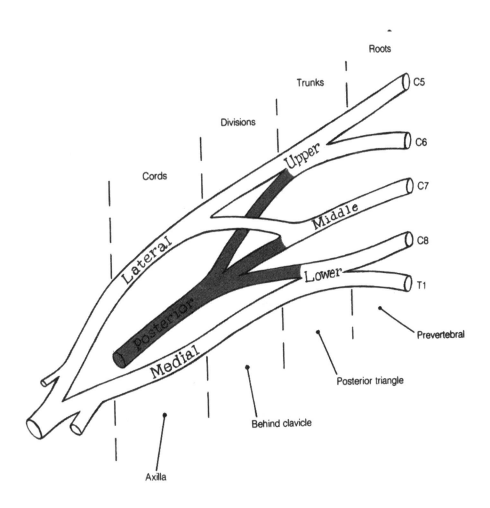

Figure 5.3

From: Hall-Craggs, E.C.B. (1990). **Anatomy as a Basis for Clinical Medicine**, 2nd edition, p. 98. Reprinted by permission of Williams and Wilkins.

Then add more details. (**Figure 5.4**)

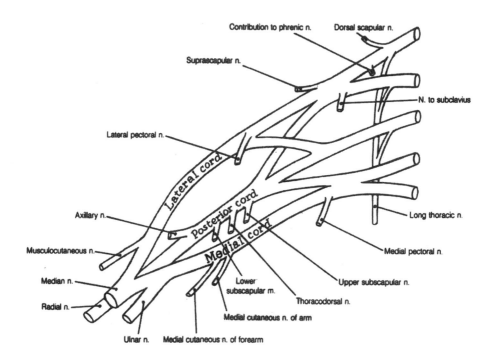

Contribution to phrenic n.   Dorsal scapular n.

Suprascapular n.

N. to subclavius

Lateral pectoral n.

Lateral cord

Posterior cord

Axillary n.

Medial cord

Long thoracic n.

Musculocutaneous n.

Medial pectoral n.

Median n.

Lower
subscapular m.

Upper subscapular n.

Radial n.

Thoracodorsal n.

Medial cutaneous n. of arm

Ulnar n.   Medial cutaneous n. of forearm

Figure 5.4

From: Hall-Craggs, E.C.B. (1990). **Anatomy as a Basis for Clinical Medicine**, 2nd edition, p. 99.
Reprinted by permission of Williams and Wilkins.

Next, fill in the rest of the details for the complete picture.

F.   Draw structures from memory to see how well you know them.

This is a crucial step, especially for success on practical examinations. For example, when you view the brachial plexus in an atlas, you may easily recognize the details. However, to see if you really know it, draw it from memory. *If you can draw it, you will be able to identify it.*

G.   Study the connections between regions.

Often, when you view plates in an atlas or dissect structures in the laboratory, you think of them in one region, usually in the region from which access to the structure is easiest. But on written examinations, test questions are not written with such constraints. On practical examinations, structures can be dissected and labeled from angles you have not anticipated. So, it is important to study the *entire* path that a structure takes and to know its relations to other structures along that path.

For example, when you dissect the hypoglossal nerve, you will likely see it from either the inferior or posterior aspect of the mandible. When studying, it is important to trace the hypoglossal nerve from its exit from the brain to its termination in the mouth, perhaps a view different from the one you saw in laboratory. Similarly, a view of the superior mesenteric artery at its branch point from the aorta looks quite different from a view of it at another point along its path. A long structure can become confusing if you have not taken the time to trace its path and note its relationships to other structures along the path. Keep questions like these in mind: "What does the radial nerve look like through the arm and forearm?" "What happens to the azygos vein in the thorax?"

H.   Consolidate and organize information.

A text passage on the brachial plexus, for example, may go on for several pages. This information will be remembered better and reviewed more easily by putting related information together in meaningful categories. **Figure 5.5** consolidates the information in chart form.

Nerve	Origin	Path	Innervates
Dorsal Scapular (C5)	C5	Pierces scalenus medius m.; passes thru posterior cervical triangle; descends deep to lev. scapulae and rhomboids	Rhomboids, levator scapulae
Long Thoracic (C5-C7)	C5-C7	Descends b/h brachial plexus and runs on external surface of the serratus anterior m.	Serratus anterior
Supra-scapular (C5, C6)	Upper trunk	Runs laterally across posterior cervical triangle; passes thru scapular notch under superior transverse scapular ligament (NOTE: suprascap. artery passes over trns. scap. lig. -- Army over bridge; Navy under it)	Supraspinatus, infraspinatus
N. Subclavius (C5, C6)	Upper trunk	Descends in front of brachial plexus and subclavian artery and b/h clavicle to reach subclavius m. (usually branches to accessory phrenic n.)	Subclavius, sterno-clavicular joint

Figure 5.5

Figure 5.6 organizes the material in outline form. You may prefer studying and learning material this way.

MEDIAN NERVE	ULNAR NERVE
Arm: • Coracobrachialis • Biceps Brachii • Brachialis Forearm: • Pronator Teres • Flexor Carpi Radialis • Palmaris Longus • Flexor Digitorum Superficialis • Flexor Pollicis Longus • Flexor Digitorum Profundus • Pronator Quadratus Hand: • All of the Thenar muscles • Abductor Pollicis Brevis • Flexor Pollicis Brevis • Opponens Pollicis • Lumbricals (for digits 2, 3)	Arm: • Nothing Forearm: • Flexor Carpi Ulnaris • Flexor Digitorum Profundus (medial half) Hand: • Palmaris Brevis • Hypothenars • Abductor Digiti Minimi • Flexor Digiti Minimi • Opponens Digiti Minimi • Lumbricals (for digits 4, 5) • Palmar Interossei • Dorsal Interossei • Abductor Pollicis

Figure 5.6

I.   Review cumulatively.

Be certain to review cumulatively as you proceed. This approach is described in detail in Chapter 3.

J.   Use Gross Anatomy laboratory time efficiently.

Time spent in Gross Anatomy laboratory can be one of the most effective methods for learning the material; however, if not utilized properly, it can become a waste of valuable time. Some suggestions to help you get the most out of laboratory are listed below:

- Preview so that you know what to expect (see Chapter 2).

- Set realistic goals for yourself. Will you remember all the structures examined in this laboratory session? Or is it better to learn one structure at a time and add to these? (see cumulative review, Chapter 3).

- Learn actively. Don't stand back and let others do all the dissecting.

- Locate structures in more than one cadaver. Structures can appear quite different from one cadaver to the next.

- Review and clarify. End each laboratory session with a review of the structures just dissected and identified. Begin the next session with a review of structures dissected and identified in the previous session.

- Set up a practice practical with a group of students. Include different cadavers in this mock test. Remember, the practical examination will have only a few questions, if any, tagged on your cadaver.

K.   Become familiar with the types of questions you will be asked.

- **Gross Anatomy questions require that you know the location or path of a structure and its relationship to other structures.**

Which of the following statements regarding the femoral triangle is true?

  (A) It contains the femoral artery, femoral vein, lymphatic vessels,
       but not the femoral nerve.
  (B) The femoral artery is lateral to the femoral nerve.
  (C) The femoral vein is lateral to the femoral nerve.
  (D) The femoral vein is lateral to the femoral artery.
  (E) It is bordered by the inguinal ligament posteriorly,
       the sartorius muscle laterally, and the adductor longus
       muscle medially.

Discussion:

The femoral triangle is an important anatomic landmark located in the upper thigh. It is bordered by the inguinal ligament superiorly, the sartorius muscle laterally, the adductor longus muscle medially, and contains the femoral artery, vein, and nerve. Answer: **E**.

  • **Gross Anatomy questions require that you understand the clinical significance of many types of injuries.**

A 25-year-old housepainter comes to see you after falling head first off a ladder, landing on his head and shoulder. On examination, you notice that he is holding his arm in an odd position. You suspect an injury to the upper trunk of the brachial plexus. Which of the following deficits is most likely?

  (A) Impairment of wrist and finger flexion, forearm pronation, and thenar
       atrophy with sensory loss of the radial 2-1/2 fingers and lateral palm.
  (B) Impairment of abduction and lateral rotation of the arm and pronation
       of the forearm without sensory loss.
  (C) Impairment of the triceps and brachioradialis reflex and wrist drop with
       loss of sensation over the forearm.
  (D) Impairment of wrist flexion and adduction with loss of sensation over the
       ulnar 1-1/2 fingers and the medial palm.
  (E) Inability to raise the arm above the horizontal and "winging" of the
       scapula without sensory loss.

Discussion:

Injury to the superior trunk of the brachial plexus (C5 and C6 roots) can occur following the displacement of the head away from the shoulder. It leads to a syndrome known as Erb-Duchenne palsy with the arm assuming a characteristic "waiter's tip" appearance. Answer: **B**.

- **Gross Anatomy questions require that you understand the basic function of a structure and are often disguised as clinical questions.**

A patient visits your office for a routine screening physical examination. On examination, you notice that she can not elevate her right eye from the abducted position. She is most likely to have dysfunction of which of the following oculomotor muscles?

- (A) Superior rectus
- (B) Inferior rectus
- (C) Lateral rectus
- (D) Superior oblique
- (E) Inferior oblique

Discussion:

The movement of the eyeball is complex. It is mediated by six oculomotor muscles working either alone or together. From an abducted position (i.e., the eye is pointing away from the body) the only muscle that can elevate the eyeball is the superior rectus muscle. Answer: **A**.

- **Gross Anatomy questions require that you understand the normal function of a structure.**

Which of the following structures lies in the endocardium in the lower part of the atrial septum and slows impulse conduction to the ventricles?

- (A) Sinoatrial (SA) node
- (B) Atrioventricular (AV) node
- (C) Atrioventricular bundle (of His)
- (D) Left bundle branch
- (E) Right bundle branch

Discussion:

After the heartbeat is initiated by the SA node, located in the right ventricle at the base of the superior vena cava, it travels to the AV node. The delay in conduction at the AV node is designed to increase the efficiency of the ventricular contraction. Answer: **B**.

- **Gross Anatomy questions may require that you know the sequence and significance of embryonic events.**

In the development of the human embryo:

    (A)   Lateral infolding occurs before the formation of the neural plate.

    (B)   The blastocyst consists of the embryoblast and the trophoblast.

    (C)   The blastocyst has formed all three germ layers.

    (D)   Somites are the anlagen of the internal viscera.

    (E)   Gastrulation occurs after the formation of the primitive streak and neural plate.

Discussion:

During development, the embryo undergoes many processes simultaneously. However, it is important to note when each of these processes begins and ends. The blastocyst, which implants into the wall of the uterus (endometrium), has two components, an embryoblast (inner cell mass), which gives rise to the embryo and fetus, and the trophoblast, which gives rise to the fetal components of the placenta and other supporting structures. Answer: **B**.

CHAPTER 6

STRATEGIES FOR STUDYING MICROSCOPIC ANATOMY

Microscopic Anatomy (Histology) focuses on organelle, cell, tissue, and organ structures as seen in the light and electron microscopes. Details of structure as seen in sections of tissues are revealed in the light and transmission electron microscope; whereas, details of surface structure are revealed in the scanning electron microscope.

Understanding the relationship between tissue structure and tissue function is the most significant task involved in learning Microscopic Anatomy. You should learn structure-function relationships so thoroughly that you can predict structure if you are given function and deduce function if you are given structure. Knowing that different organs have groups of cells with similar structure if they have similar function will simplify the task of learning how to identify different organs. For example, the exocrine pancreas and the parotid salivary gland both release protein-rich secretions into the lumen of the digestive system. Both organs have many microscopic similarities, e.g., pyramidal acini with basal rough endoplasmic reticulum and apical zymogen granules. Often, different cells, tissues, and organs must be compared and contrasted to one another.

Microscopic Anatomy also provides a basis for understanding tissue pathology and is therefore clinically relevant. Later in your studies, it will do you little good to learn that malignant cells have pleomorphic nuclei if you don't have a sense of the limits of normal nuclear morphology.

One key to success in Microscopic Anatomy is to use different sources of information, including inspection of sections in the light microscope, reading textbooks, studying illustrations in an atlas, and using some of the excellent CD-ROM collections of images that come with some atlases.

Chapter Overview

A. Understand the relationship between structural and functional qualities in tissues.
B. Integrate sources of visual information to learn Microscopic Anatomy more effectively.
C. Learn the fundamentals.
D. Use verbal cues to identify the structural and functional characteristics that distinguish one tissue from another.
E. Pay special attention to look-alikes. Utilize compare and contrast strategies.
F. Learn to study a new slide.
G. Prepare systematically for the practical examination.
H. Become familiar with the types of written examination questions you will be asked.
I. Become familiar with the format of your practical examination.

A. Understand the relationship between structural and functional qualities in tissues.

Just as in Gross Anatomy, where structure and function are related, there is an important relationship between structure and function in Microscopic Anatomy. Pay attention to this relationship when you study because cells and tissues with structural similarities possess functional similarities as well. For example, virtually all cells that perform exocrine secretion of protein (e.g., lipase from the pancreas or α-amylase from the parotid glands) have common structural features...euchromatic nuclei with prominent nucleoli, basal abundance of rough endoplasmic reticulum, and many mitochondria.

Noting the similarities between structure and function will make recognizing and identifying various tissues easier. The ultimate goal is to be able to describe the function if given the structure and to be able to describe structure if you know the function.

B. Integrate sources of visual information to learn Microscopic Anatomy more effectively.

When reading text that describes a structure, look at a picture of that structure as you are reading its description from the text. Be sure that you can identify the described features and that you understand their functional role. For example, **Figure 6.1** shows the reticular fibers present in lymph nodes. As you read a text description of reticular fibers as fine collagenous fibers, look at the picture of the section of a lymph node stained with a special silver stain to reveal argyrophilic (silver-loving) fibers. Furthermore, **Figure 6.1** illustrates the essential connection between text and pictorials. As you read about the reticular fibers, be sure to identify the visual features in the accompanying figure that illustrate the characteristics described in the text.

> **Figure 6.1** is a light micrograph of the cortex of a lymph node showing **reticular fibers** (black structures at arrows). Reticular fibers are abundant surrounding glandular acini, between smooth muscle cells, and in the lamina propria of distensible organs in the gastrointestinal tract and the reproductive system. They also form a complex supportive network in lymph nodes, the spleen, and the liver. Reticular fibers are approximately 1.0 μm in diameter and consist of type-III collagen and associated proteoglycans whose carbohydrates make them stain black when treated with silver salts (i.e., they are **argyrophilic**).

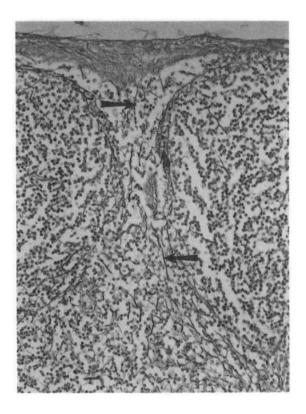

Figure 6.1

C.   Learn the fundamentals.

In most traditional courses in Microscopic Anatomy, the material is additive so it is important to learn the fundamentals early in the course. The identification of different tissue types is crucial to the later identification of specific organs. For example, learn the differences between the varieties of general and specialized connective tissues and learn to distinguish bundles of nerve fibers, smooth muscle, and connective tissue. Later on when studying the gastrointestinal tract, you will learn that one of the differences between the small intestine and the large intestine is in the way the smooth muscle of the muscularis externa is arranged. To make this differentiation, you will have to have already learned how to distinguish smooth muscle from adjacent connective tissue.

Another important fundamental skill for Microscopic Anatomy is the ability to imagine three-dimensional structures and tissues from their two-dimensional representation in thin sections. For example, a simple tubular organ can look circular on a slide cut perpendicular to its long axis (perpendicular cross-section), oval if cut obliquely (oblique cross-section), or elongated like a stalk if cut longitudinally (longitudinal section). When a villus is sectioned parallel to its long axis, it will appear as a finger-like projection with a connective tissue core covered by an epithelial layer. In contrast, when the plane of section is perpendicular to the long axis of the villus, the same structure will now appear as a central circular core of connective tissue surrounded by a ring of epithelium.

Learning early on to consider the *orientation* of the specimen when looking at slides will enhance your ability to identify structures later in the course.

D.   Use verbal cues to identify the structural and functional characteristics that distinguish one tissue from another.

To learn a cell or tissue type, say out loud the characteristics of each. Answer the following questions: What color does it stain? Are there special stains used? What is/are the shape(s) of the cell(s)? Is there a nucleus present? If so, where is it located? What is its relative size? What is its shape? What organelles (if any) are prominent? Repeat this process for every slide of the same tissue type.

As you learn other cell and tissue types, state the characteristics of the new cell or tissue and also state the features that distinguish the second cell or tissue type from the first. Answer these questions when comparing and contrasting the two types to each other: How are the cells/tissues/organs in this set the same? How are they different? Repeat this process for every slide as you add new material. As you go on to a third cell or tissue type, be certain to compare and contrast *both* of the previous types you studied.

An example of this method applied to a comparative study of muscular tissue would proceed in three steps. First, look at a slide of skeletal muscle and say: "This is skeletal muscle because it has nuclei on the periphery of cells, it is striated, and it has long, mostly straight, unbranched fibers. Each cell (fiber) is a multinucleate structure with many nuclei in each fiber." Repeat this process for several slides of skeletal muscle until you can easily recognize all slides of skeletal muscle and have learned the significant and unique structural features of skeletal muscle.

Next look at several slides of smooth muscle and for each one say: "This is smooth muscle because each fusiform, nonstriated cell has a centrally placed nucleus." Continue with: "This is **NOT** skeletal muscle because smooth muscle has a single centrally placed nucleus in each cell while skeletal muscle has many peripherally placed nuclei in each cell; and smooth muscle is nonstriated while skeletal muscle is striated."

Finally, as you move on to cardiac muscle, say: "This is cardiac muscle because each striated cell has a centrally placed nucleus and shorter, often branched fibers. It is **NOT** skeletal muscle because skeletal muscle has peripherally placed nuclei and long, straight, multinucleate fibers. It is **NOT** smooth muscle because it is clearly striated."

E. Pay special attention to look-alikes. Utilize compare and contrast strategies.

Many cells, tissues, and organs look quite similar, especially to a novice. Therefore, it is essential to focus on the unique features that distinguish them from one another. Compare look-alikes side by side, attending carefully to features that differentiate them. For example, peripheral nerve tissue often resembles smooth muscle tissue or dense irregular connective tissue. **Figure 6.2** clearly compares and contrasts some sample look-alikes. The items in bold are features that can be used to distinguish similar tissues.

Comparison of Tissues

Dense Irregular Connective Tissue	Smooth Muscle Tissue	Peripheral Nerve Tissue
• many fibers, many directions • **few nuclei**	• many fibers, many directions • **many nuclei**	• many fibers, **parallel** • many nuclei

Figure 6.2

Figures 6.3 and **6.4** compare and contrast the often-confused, similar-looking glands of the oral cavity.

Glands of the Oral Cavity		
Gland	Structure	Type of Acini
Parotid	• Acini, ducts, connective tissue (CT), and nerves. The CT extends septa that divide the gland into lobules. Adipose tissue MAY be present	• **Serous acini (98%)** • Have extensive, basally-located RER, prominent Golgi, and apically-positioned, membrane-bound secretory granules. Nuclei more centrally placed.
Submandibular	• Contains serous and mucous acini. Has **serous demilunes**	• **Serous and mucous acini** (if you see both, think submand.). Serous stain blue/violet. Mucous stain lighter, have basal nuclei.
Sublingual	• Mucous and serous acini • Lots of CT	• **Contains almost all mucous acini.** • Mucous and serous acini can be interspersed or in separate regions.

Figure 6.3

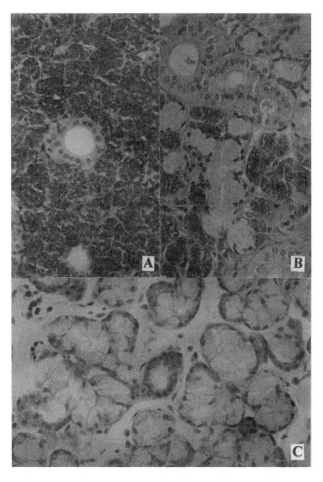

Figure 6.4 Light micrographs of parotid (A) (mostly serous acini); submandibular (B) (serous and mucous acini); sublingual (C) (mostly mucous acini) glands.

F.   Learn to study a new slide.

The steps for studying a new slide are listed below.

1. **If the slide is labeled, recall whatever information from Gross Anatomy you may have already learned.** Ask questions, e.g., "Should the structure look like a circle with a central opening? Should it look like a densely packed, solid structure?"

2. **Examine the slide with the naked eye against a white background.** Look for any structural details that can be discerned with no magnification.

3. **With the lowest power objective available on your microscope, scan all of the regions of the specimen.** Take your time to be sure that you have covered all the salient features.

4. **Go back at a higher power and study each region, looking for features of the specimen that a) place it in a certain organ system and b) identify it as a specific tissue.** Learning the features that group organs together as well as the features that are specific for a particular organ will make identification easier.

For example, if you were studying a slide of the duodenum, your steps would be similar to those listed below.

1. Recall whatever information from Gross Anatomy that you may have already learned. The duodenum is a circular structure with a central cavity (lumen).

2. Examine the slide with the naked eye. You should be able to see the circular structure with the central cavity (lumen) that you are expecting. You should also be able to see the muscularis externa and the mucosa. Mucosal villi will be visible.

3. With the lowest power objective available on your microscope, scan all of the regions of the specimen. Be sure to scan the entire slide to catch all the salient features of the duodenum.

4. Go back at a higher power and study each region, looking for features of the specimen that a) place it in a certain organ system and b) identify it as a specific tissue.

a) Study the luminal epithelium (simple columnar). The mucosal luminal epithelium will consist of a predominance of simple columnar absorptive cells with a scattered population of goblet cells among the columnar absorptive cells.

b) Examine the lamina propria of villi to find important features, e.g., wispy slips of smooth muscle, fibroblasts, lacteals, plasma cells, and lymphocytes.

c) Locate the muscularis mucosae, a thin layer of smooth muscle cells between the loose irregular connective tissue of the lamina propria on the luminal (mucosal) side and the loose irregular connective tissue beneath it. The muscularis mucosae is the deepest layer of the mucosa. Between it and the muscularis externa, one finds a connective tissue domain called the submucosa.

d) Notice that there is a large amount of glandular material in the submucosa. This is a unique feature of the duodenum. If you know from Gross Anatomy that the duodenum is the first part of the small intestine, receiving acidic chyme from the stomach, it will be easier to recall that the duodenum has submucosal Brunner glands, which secrete mucus (to protect the duodenal mucosa from gastric acid) and bicarbonate (to neutralize acidic chyme).

e) Study the smooth muscle layers in the muscularis externa. The inner layer is circular and the outer layer is longitudinal with respect to the long axis of the duodenum. Once you have found the muscularis mucosae and the muscularis externa, it will be easier to locate components of the Meissner plexus, just deep to the muscularis mucosae, and the Auerbach plexus, between the inner circular and outer longitudinal layers of the muscularis externa.

This strategy for studying a new slide should also be used when you are analyzing an unknown on an examination.

G.   Prepare systematically for the practical examination.

Systematic preparation for the practical examination will help you to capitalize on the time you spend studying and will make for more effective recall. Below are some steps to help you organize your practical examination preparation.

1.   **First, view slides in sets to identify common features.** For example, when studying the gastrointestinal tract, view some slides from each area to review all the characteristics common to each.

2.   **Go through the slides again, this time noting all the differences between the various regions of the organ system.** For example, when viewing the GI tract, note that duodenal villi (the stalks projecting into the lumen) are short and fat whereas jejunal villi are long and flat. Similarly, you will learn that the duodenum has Brunner glands whereas the jejunum does not.

3.   **Consider the different functions of the elements of the organ system to help you make distinctions.** For instance, in the GI tract, the esophagus is really a simple conduit for food from the mouth to the stomach, hence, its lining is specialized to resist abrasion. It is lined with flattened cells piled one on top of the other (called stratified squamous epithelium). In contrast, the small intestine does most of the digestion and absorption and so is lined with cells specific for these purposes (columnar absorptive epithelium with goblet cells). Each area's function dictates its structure.

4.   **As the examination approaches, select slides randomly from more than one organ system.** A study partner can be helpful in setting up this mock practical examination. If you will be allowed to do so in your real exam, begin by examining the slide with your naked eye first to look for gross diagnostic features. Then begin your systematic review of the slide as described above to make the identification.

5.   **Avoid the common mistake of jumping too quickly to identification without finishing your systematic examination of the slide.** Once you have convinced yourself of the answer, it is easy to also convince yourself that something you see on the slide supports your answer when in fact it does not. Your thinking might progress along lines like these:

     a)   This is part of the GI tract.

     b)   It has villi and is therefore part of the small intestine.

     c)   It has Brunner glands and is therefore duodenum.

     d)   Confirm your identification by looking for other features specific only to the duodenum, e.g., short villi.

Preparing for the practical examination in this way will keep you from having to memorize a long laundry list of features for each specific organ. You will only need to know information that is common to the group of organs and then some other details that distinguish the particular organs of that group from each other. Being systematic will increase your accuracy, and thus, it will increase your test scores.

H. Become familiar with the types of written examination questions you will be asked.

- **Microscopic Anatomy questions require that you learn to recognize and identify cells and subcellular structures.**

What structure(s) is (are) identified by the arrows in the light micrograph of a silver-stained specimen shown in **Figure 6.1**?

- (A) Reticular fibers
- (B) Elastic fibers
- (C) Collagen fibers
- (D) Basement membranes
- (E) Intermediate filaments and microtubules

Discussion:

As shown in **Figure 6.1**, reticular fibers form a delicate supporting framework and are found in glandular tissue, smooth muscle, lymph nodes, the spleen, and the liver. They are made up of type III collagen and proteoglycans. They stain black when treated with silver salts. Answer: **A**.

- **Microscopic Anatomy questions require that you understand the microscopic organization of cells, tissues, and organs.**

Which of the following statements about the sarcomere is true?

- (A) Thick filaments contain primarily actin.
- (B) Thin filaments contain primarily myosin.
- (C) The thick and thin filaments are perpendicular to the contraction direction.
- (D) Thick and thin filaments do not overlap in the I and H bands.
- (E) During contraction, the A band shortens.

Discussion:

Striated muscle cells contain contractile proteins arranged in contractile units called sarcomeres. Sarcomeres contain thick filaments (mainly myosin aggregates) and thin filaments (mainly actin globular proteins arranged in two long chains intertwined like two strands of pearls). During muscle contraction, these filaments slide past one another, causing sarcomeres to shorten. This ATP-dependent process is called the sliding filament mechanism of muscle contraction. Answer: **D**.

- **Microscopic Anatomy questions require that you understand the functional qualities of cells and structures.**

Which of the following types of epithelia is best suited to accommodate reversible changes in surface area and contact with potentially noxious compounds?

   (A)   Pseudostratified ciliated columnar

   (B)   Startified squamous, keratinized

   (C)   Transitional

   (D)   Simple cuboidal

   (E)   Simple columnar, ciliated

Discussion:

Epithelium is one of the four basic tissue types, along with connective tissue, muscular tissue, and nervous tissue. Epithelia cover surfaces and line cavities. They serve as barriers and boundaries. Transitional epithelium, which lines the renal calyces, ureter, urinary bladder, and upper part of the urethra, is specialized to accommodate changes in surface area (e.g., when the bladder is distended by urine) and the potentially noxious urine contained in the lumen of the urinary bladder. Answer: **C**.

I.   Become familiar with the format of your practical examination.

Each of the different examination styles require that you be able to make rapid, accurate interpretations of complex visual images.

1.   You may experience an examination with many stations, and a short time limit allotted for each. These may consist of a large number of slides, photographs, and/or projected color slides that must be identified quickly. Answers usually consist of either a simple identification or an identification with brief statements about function.

2.   Some examinations consist of identical sets of examination materials given to all students at the same time, with a time limit for the entire examination. In this kind of examination, all students are given a set of slides, micrographs, and diagrams. The slides are very similar (usually serial sections from the same region of the same tissue specimen), and the

photographs are usually duplicates. Students are typically required to identify structures, and they may be required to list observational criteria used to make the identification based on real observations from their own slide. They may also be required to supply functional information about the organ.

3. Another examination format consists of slides or digital graphic files being projected onto a screen. Students are required to identify what they see within a short time frame. Students may also be required to provide brief functional descriptions of labeled structures in projected images.

4. Another way to test students is to provide a natural specimen where there are several different organs cut in section. Students are then required to identify organs by location and structural details. Some professors also create artificial collections of organs embedded in one block of paraffin, without the benefit of their normal anatomic context. Students are required to identify organs, list criteria for identification, and provide information about function.

Professors typically make it clear what kind of examination to expect. In many medical schools, more advanced students will organize mock practicals (often with faculty approval and assistance) to help you over the hurdles of the unfamiliar format of practical examinations.

CHAPTER 7

STRATEGIES FOR STUDYING BEHAVIORAL SCIENCE AND PSYCHIATRY

Behavioral Science and **Psychiatry** both involve the study of psychosocial processes. **Behavioral Science** focuses on the major theories of personality organization, psychosocial development, progression through the lifecycle, the emotional, cultural, and social determinates of disease, and the role of the doctor-patient relationship in the context of the health care delivery system. **Psychiatry** focuses on mental illnesses, their genetic and biochemical bases, and the different modalities (medications/counseling) used to treat them. Many medical students have had some exposure to this material in sociology and psychology courses in college. Some material overlaps with topics introduced in Pharmacology (treatment for mental illnesses and substance ingestion/withdrawal), and Neuroscience (diseases with causes known to involve neurological impairment.)

Chapter Overview

A. Develop a framework for the material.

B. Learn terminology in a meaningful way. The words will often direct you.

C. Use charts and diagrams to consolidate and organize information and to aid in summarizing.

D. Pay attention to "differences" and the "unexpected."

E. Use mnemonics to aid recall.

F. Become familiar with the types of examination questions you will be asked.

A.   Develop a framework for the material.

You are likely to be assigned a textbook for this course. Before you begin reading, look at your textbook to see how the material is organized. In Psychiatry much of the material presented is organized according to the *Diagnostic and Statistical Manual of Mental Disorders, 4th edition (DSM-IV)*. The *DSM-IV* is logically divided into sections such as, "mood disorders", "anxiety disorders" and "substance-related disorders." Each of these large, general sections is then subdivided into specific disorders based on the presence, duration, and course of various signs and symptoms, as illustrated in **Figure 7.1**. For example, the section on mood disorders is divided into *depressive disorders, bipolar disorders, and other mood disorders* based on the constellation of symptoms. The Depressive Disorders are then subdivided based on the duration and course of the symptoms into *major depressive disorder and dsythymic disorder*. Paying attention to this framework will enhance acquisition by establishing a big picture on which to "hang" further details.

MOOD DISORDERS

Depressive Disorders

Major Depressive Disorder

Dysthymic Disorder

Bipolar Disorders

Bipolar I Disorder

Bipolar II Disorder

Cyclothymic Disorder

Other Mood Disorders

Mood Disorder due to a general medical condition, e.g., heart disease, renal failure, cancer, etc.

Substance-Induced Mood Disorder

---

*Adapted from American Psychiatric Association (1994). *Diagnostic and Statistical Manual of Mental Disorders*, fourth edition.

Figure 7.1

B.   Learn terminology in a meaningful way. The words will often direct you.

The terminology used in the specific identification of psychiatric disorders often overlaps with that used in everyday speech. As a result, the names of specific disorders are often descriptive and can be used to predict the specific constellations of symptoms expected. For example, *major* depressive disorder refers to the development of one or more episodes of *severe depression*, i.e., marked sadness, sleep disturbances, decreased ability to concentrate, and changes in appetite and weight. *Bipolar* disorder refers to someone with a history of both depressive and manic episodes, i.e., they have had episodes on *both polar ends* of the mood spectrum. However, it is important to pay close attention, as distinctions can often be subtle and confusing. For example, *cyclo*thymic disorder is similar to bipolar disorder because it refers to someone with periods of abnormally depressed and elevated mood. However, cyclothymic disorder implies more rapid *cycling* between them.

C.   Use charts and diagrams to consolidate and organize information and to aid in summarizing.

Information can be effectively summarized using charts and diagrams to help classify material and remember distinctions between things. The chart in **Figure 7.2** may be helpful when studying lifecycle and development.

D.   Pay attention to "differences" and the "unexpected."

When information is consolidated into charts and tables, patterns and associations become more evident, and commonalties can be noted. However, it is of particular value to pay attention to "unexpected" information and relationships, as these things are more easily remembered. For example, *schizotypal personality disorder* and *schizoid personality disorder* are two separate entities that both describe socially isolated individuals. However, schizotypal individuals often display unusual affect, exhibit eccentric patterns of thinking (they may be obsessed with metaphysical, occult, or

AGE	MAJOR TASKS/ISSUES	DEVELOPMENTAL THEORIES
Infant	Formation of intimate attachment Stranger anxiety	Trust vs. Mistrust (Erikson) Oral phase (Freud)
Toddler	Separate from the primary caregiver (mother) Separation anxiety	Autonomy vs. Doubt (Erikson) Anal phase (Freud)
Preschool	Increasing vocabulary, imagination May have imaginary friends Interest in sex differences Formation of conscience	Initiative vs. Guilt (Erikson) Phallic/oedipal phase (Freud)
Puberty	Peers become more important than family Prefer same-sex friends Logical thought develops	Industry vs. Inferiority (Erikson) Latency phase (Freud)
Adolescence	Sexual development (puberty) Formation of personality Abstract thought develops	Identity vs. Role Confusion (Erikson) Genital phase (Freud)
Early adult	Financial and emotional independance Development of an intimate relationship May marry and have children	Intimacy vs. Isolation (Erikson) Age of transition (Levinson)
Adult	Time of great satisfaction May have social and economic power Menopause	Generativity vs. Stagnation (Erikson) 'Midlife crisis' (Levinson)
Late adult	Strength and physical health decline Loss of friends and family May develop depression	Ego Integrity vs. Despair (Erikson) 5 stages of dying (Kubler-Ross)

Figure 7.2

religious phenomena) and have odd manners of speech. Schizoid individuals tend to be emotionally distant and seemingly derive little joy from living, but have normal thought processes. To distinguish these entities, it may be useful to think of schizo*typal* patients as having a mild type of schizophrenia, while schiz*oid* patients may think normally but desire to avoid personal interactions. In **Figures 7.3, 7.4 and 7.5** major differences between similar disorders are noted in boldface type.

Cluster A- These people are often described as being "Odd and Eccentric"

PERSONALITY DISORDER	DESCRIPTIVE CHARACTERISTICS	DISTINGUISHING FEATURES
Paranoid	Distrustful and suspicious of others Often secretive and socially isolated Emotionally cold	**May have periods of psychosis with persecutory delusions** May worsen with age
Schizoid	Avoid personal interactions Seem to derive little joy from living Indifferent to compliments/criticisms Associated with schizophrenia	**Not lonely, does not mind being isolated** **No psychosis or thought disturbance** May choose occupation that minimizes contact with others
Schizotypal	Avoid personal interactions Uncomfortable with social relationships Associated with schizophrenia	**Odd patterns of thinking** **Odd manners of speech and appearance**

Figure 7.3

Cluster B- These people have a tendency towards the "Dramatic and Erratic"

PERSONALITY DISORDER	DESCRIPTIVE CHARACTERISTICS	DISTINGUISHING FEATURES
Antisocial	Tend to cheat, lie, steal, and fight Violate the rights of others without remorse Manipulate others to serve their ends	**Often in social strife with criminal records** Likely male May lessen with age
Borderline	Unstable mood and behavior Impulsive and self-destructive Unstable relationships, emotions, and self image	**Lives tend to be characterized by chaos, disorder, and suicide attempts** Likely female May lessen with age
Histrionic	Emotionally shallow with increased emotional liability Inappropriately seductive and over-romantic	**Seeks attention** Likely female May lessen with age
Narcissistic	Overriding sense of grandiosity and entitlement Preoccupied with self-described accomplishments Hypersensitive to real or imagined slights	**Demand excessive attention and the "best" treatment** Likely male May worsen with age

Figure 7.4

Cluster C- These people are often noticeably "Fearful and Anxious"

PERSONALITY DISORDER	DESCRIPTIVE CHARACTERISTICS	DISTINGUISHING FEATURES
Avoidant	Avoid personal interacts because of fear of rejection Low self esteem and feelings of inadequacy	**Feels lonely, but isolates self from others because of fear of rejection** May lessen with age
Dependent	Participate in few independent activities Submissive and "clingy" behavior Low self-esteem	**Feels lonely, but seeks closeness with others and desires to be taken care of**
Obsessive-Compulsive	Preoccupation with orderliness and details at the expense of the overall goal Concerned with perfection and control	**Difficulty with interpersonal relationships because they are strict, inflexible, perfectionists** May be miserly and refuse to give up worthless possessions Likely male

Figure 7.5

E.   Use mnemonics to aid recall.

Mnemonics can sometimes be useful in aiding memory. The common depressive symptoms seen in major depressive disorder can be remembered using the mnemonic "**SADNESS**": **S**leep, **A**ppetite, **D**ysphoria, a**N**hedonia, **E**nergy, **S**uicide, **S**ex. People suffering from major depression often complain of insomnia/hypersomnia, increased or decreased appetite for food (with associated weight gain/loss), dysphoria and sadness, anhedonia (decreased ability to derive pleasure from activities), decreased energy, recurrent thoughts of death or suicide, and a decreased libido. The symptoms typical of a manic episode can be remembered using the mnemonic "**BIPOLAR**": **B**labber, **I**nsomnia, **P**oor judgement, g**O**als, **L**ofty, **A**ggressive, **R**acing thoughts. People suffering from a manic episode are often aggressive and exhibit increased speech, racing thoughts, decreased need for sleep, increased goal directed activity, inflated self-esteem.

F.   Become familiar with the types of examination questions you will be asked.

- **Behavioral science questions require that you have a basic understanding of the health care system in the United States.**

Which of the following statements about Medicare is true?

(A) It is primarily designed for people over 65 or those with disabilities.

(B) It is primarily designed for poor people and pays for all medical costs.

(C) It is primarily designed for children under the age of 12.

(D) It covers all health care costs including inpatient, prescription drug, nursing home, and outpatient expenses.

(E) It is administered through the Food and Drug Administration (FDA).

Discussion:

Medicare, financed and managed under the Social Security Administration, was primarily designed for people over the age of 65 or for individuals with permanent disabilities. Medicaid is designed for people with low incomes and is funded by federal and state governments. Answer: **A**.

- **Behavioral science questions require knowledge of normal development and lifecycle processes.**

Which of the following developmental markers characterize early adulthood (approximately 20 to 40 years of age)?

(A) A sense of pride and satisfaction in life's accomplishments and the recognition that all options are no longer available.

(B) A continued sense of productivity and a significant change in work or personal relationships.

(C) The building of intimate relationships and a period of reappraisal of one's life.

(D) Reaching the climacterium and the resulting decrease in physiologic and psychologic function.

(E) The completion of the formation of a sense of conscience and the acquisition of logical thought.

Discussion:

During the period of early adulthood, independence develops and biologic development reaches its peak. Erikson calls this the stage of intimacy vs. isolation; the major task is to develop an intimate relationship with another person lest one suffer emotional isolation. Therefore, this is the period when most people marry, have children, and begin families. Answer: **C**.

- **Psychiatry questions require that you understand the major features of a variety of personality disorders and mental illnesses.**

A manic episode is defined as a distinct period of abnormally and persistently elevated, expansive, or irritable mood that lasts at least one week. During this period, patients often exhibit decreased sleep, pressured speech, and:

(A)   Increased anxiety

(B)   Decreased goal-directed activity

(C)   Grandiosity

(D)   Feelings of guilt and remorse

(E)   Depressed mood

Discussion:

Manic episodes, as seen in bipolar disorder, are associated with rapid, excited speech, decreased need for sleep, and feelings of inflated self-importance (grandiosity). During these episodes, patients may be euphoric, excitable, and hyperactive, show poor judgement, and have delusions of intelligence, strength, and power. Answer: **C.**

A 50-year-old businessman is seen in your office for an initial patient visit. He states that he came to see you because he heard that you were quite famous and that he "only sees the best" given his role as the head of "a very large company." He has not returned to his former physician after she recommended having surgery to remove an invasive skin cancer from his arm. The most likely personality disorder this patient is exhibiting is:

(A)   Histrionic

(B)   Compulsive

(C)   Dependent

(D)   Schizotypal

(E)   Narcissistic

Discussion:

People with narcissistic personality disorder have a sense of self-importance and entitlement and feel that their stature requires that they receive the absolute "best." They may risk death to avoid a potentially disfiguring surgery. Answer: **E.**

- **Psychiatry questions may require that you understand the treatment of various types of mental illness.**

Which of the following statements regarding the antipsychotic drugs is true?

(A)   All classes are equally effective against both the positive and negative features of schizophrenia.

(B)   Effects are usually seen within 24 hours of administration.

(C)   They are associated with many adverse effects, at least one of which may be fatal.

(D)   When treatment is discontinued, patients rarely relapse.

(E)   There is no role for other treatment modalities, such as behavioral therapy or family counseling.

Discussion:

Although often effective (after a 4-6 week trial period), antipsychotic drugs are associated with many adverse effects ranging from weight gain, impotence, tremor, rigidity, and other movement disorders. A rare complication is neuroleptic malignant syndrome, which can be fatal. Unfortunately, a majority of patients relapse within 18 months after discontinuing treatment. Answer: **C**.

Notes

CHAPTER 8

STRATEGIES FOR STUDYING BIOCHEMISTRY

Biochemistry is the study of the chemical reactions that take place inside the body. It involves both normal and abnormal processes, both intra- and extracellular processes, such as digestion, the immune responses, and genetic disorders. A key to success is to gain a good conceptual understanding of these processes as this will help you assimilate the necessary details more easily. If you understand the end result of a biochemical pathway and how it is linked to other pathways, learning the details will be easier. In addition, focusing on clinically relevant examples will make these details more understandable and meaningful and thereby more memorable.

Chapter Overview

A. Learn enzyme nomenclature as it is often functionally significant and descriptive.

B. Get the big picture first.

C. Identify the relationship between specific reactions and organ systems.

D. Learn biochemical pathways hierarchically.

E. Draw pathways from memory to test knowledge.

F. Work toward integration and linking.

G. Become familiar with the types of examination questions you will be asked.

A. Learn enzyme nomenclature as it is often functionally significant and descriptive.

A few examples will illustrate this often overlooked point. As in many of the complex disciplines involved in medical education, early mastery of a few fundamental concepts will facilitate learning and retention of vast amounts of material.

1. **Oxidoreductase**s catalyze reversible oxidation-reduction reactions, adding or removing hydrogen from substrates using donor/acceptor molecules such as NADH/NAD+. For example, alcohol dehydrogenase oxidizes alcohol to aldehyde by transferring 2 H from alcohol to NAD+, forming an aldehyde, NADH, and H+.

2. **Transferases** shuttle functional groups between donors and acceptors. For example, aminotransferases transfer the amino from an amino acid donor to a keto acid acceptor, producing a new amino acid and a new keto acid.

3. **Kinases** are specialized transferases that catalyze the transfer of phosphoryl groups from a nucleotide to an —OH- or —NH2-containing acceptor. For example, glucokinase transfers a —PO4 from ATP to glucose, producing ADP and glucose-6-phosphate.

4. **Hydrolases** are another special group of transferases in which the acceptor is water. For example, peptidases are a kind of hydrolase that catalyze cleavage of peptide bonds.

5. **Ligases** join smaller molecules together into larger molecules at the expense of energy-rich phosphate bonds such as those found in ATP. For example, amino acyl tRNAs are formed by ligases (synthetases) that couple amino acids to tRNA at the expense of ATP.

6. **Isomerases** catalyze isomerization reactions. For example, phosphoglucose isomerase converts glucose 6-phosphate into an isomer, fructose 6-phosphate in the glycolytic pathway.

B.   Get the big picture first.

Gain an overall conceptual picture as the initial step toward making things meaningful. Learn how one pathway relates to other biochemical pathways. Learn the basic function of the pathway. Understand beginning and end points and the overall metabolic consequences of changes in the dynamics of a pathway. This strategy will facilitate a better understanding of the disease mechanisms, clinical laboratory tests, and drug effects. An overview or introduction, as can be found in many textbooks, can be especially useful for helping you establish this basis. For example, the overview shown in **Figure 8.1** and subsequent text provides a conceptual picture of the biochemical pathways involved in carbohydrate metabolism.

Overview

"The major pathways of carbohydrate metabolism either begin or end with glucose (**Figure 8.1**). This chapter will describe the utilization of glucose as a source of energy, the formation of glucose from noncarbohydrate precursors, the storage of glucose in the form of glycogen for later use, and the release of glucose from this storage form for use by cells. An understanding of the pathways and their regulation is necessary because of the important role played by glucose in the body. Glucose is the major form in which carbohydrate absorbed from the intestinal tract is presented to cells of the body. Glucose is the only fuel used to any significant extent by a few specialized cells, and it is the major fuel used by the brain. Indeed, glucose is so important to these specialized cells and the brain that several of the major tissues of the body work together to ensure a continuous supply of this essential substrate. Glucose metabolism is defective in two very common metabolic disorders, obesity and diabetes, which in turn are contributing factors in the development of a number of major medical problems, including atherosclerosis, hypertension, small vessel disease, kidney disease, and blindness."

From: Devlin, T.M. (1992) Textbook of Biochemistry with Clinical Correlations, 3rd edition, p. 292. Reprinted by permission of John Wiley & Sons.

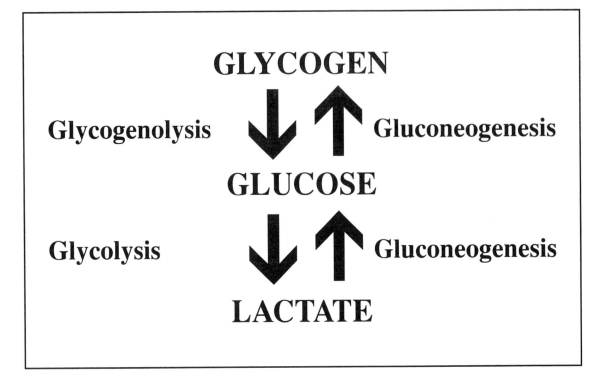

Figure 8.1

C. Identify the relationship between specific reactions and organ systems.

Note whether reactions are confined to particular organs (e.g., thyroxine production) or are almost universal throughout the body (e.g., glycolysis). Some diseases are specifically associated with one or a few organs. In other cases, diseases may have a systemic manifestation. Knowing the extent of a biochemical defect with respect to different organ systems will allow you to make a better evaluation of the clinical implications of failures in such pathways.

D. Learn biochemical pathways hierarchically.

Biochemistry forms a foundation for the understanding of metabolic pathways. There are a large number of detailed steps involved in the entire metabolic pathway. It is

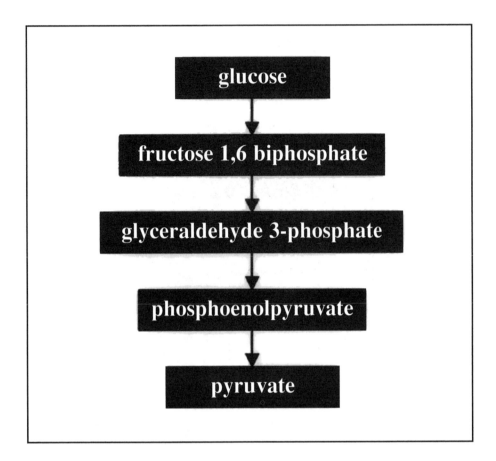

Figure 8.2

best to learn this sequence by focusing on *major* steps first, and more detailed steps thereafter. The schematic presented in **Figure 8.2** illustrates the major steps of glycolysis.

In **Figure 8.2**, only the major steps in glycolysis are listed. Glucose is the starting point of the cycle and *fructose 1,6-bisphosphate* is the main regulating step of the pathway. *Glyceraldehyde 3-phosphate* is the point at which the 6 carbon molecule of glucose is split into two 3 carbon molecules as the pathway proceeds. *Phosphoenolpyruvate* is the second to last step, and is important because it is the last reversible step in the pathway leading back up to glucose (gluconeogenesis). Once *pyruvate* has been made, remaking glucose via this path requires going into the citric acid cycle (to oxaloacetate). Once you have learned these major components of glycolysis, you should add the next level of detail, the intermediate steps, as shown in **Figure 8.3**. The major steps (from **Figure 8.2**) are highlighted in the black boxes.

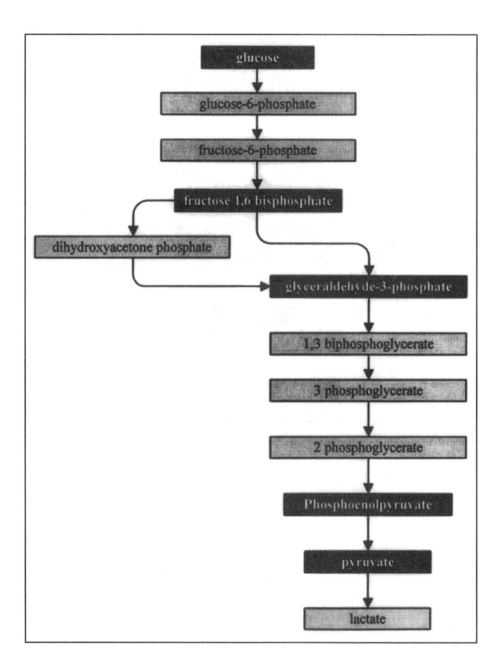

Figure 8.3

The final step in learning glycolysis will involve adding the important enzymes, regulators, and energy transfers, the next level of detail, as shown in **Figure 8.4**. Again, note that previously learned material is highlighted in black or shaded.

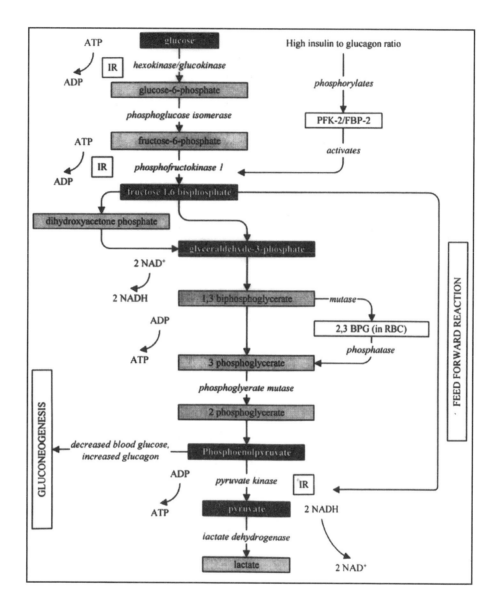

Figure 8.4

E.   Draw pathways from memory to test knowledge.

To make sure you really know each of the steps involved in a pathway, draw the pathway from memory. For example, when learning glycolysis, test your knowledge by drawing the components of the pathway. Use abbreviations for the longer terms as illustrated in **Figure 8.5**.

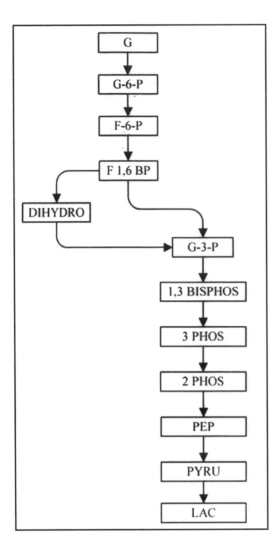

Figure 8.5

Check back to see which details you misidentified or omitted. Each time you learn another level of detail, test your knowledge by drawing out the entire structure or sequence from memory.

F. Work toward integration and linking.

Though the metabolic cycles are often taught separately, it is essential to understand how the pathways are linked. This helps lead to better retention and will also help you make predictions about what will happen to one pathway if another pathway is disrupted in some way. This is often critical to success on examinations. For example, think about how glycolysis and the citric acid cycle are related, glycolysis and the urea cycle, and so on. Study with this focus in mind and consider creating review materials that help consolidate the primary features of these interrelationships. **Figure 8.6**, for example, presents a concise summary of the metabolic relationships of fatty acids.

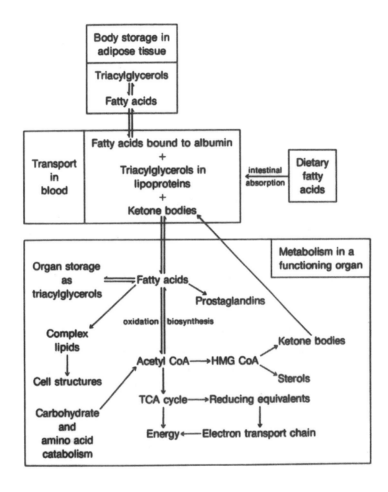

Figure 8.6

From: Devlin, T.M. (1992). **Textbook of Biochemistry with Clinical Correlations**, 3rd edition, p. 389. Reprinted by permission of John Wiley & Sons.

G. Become familiar with the types of examination questions you will be asked.

- **Biochemistry questions require that you understand the characteristics of a molecule, bond, enzyme, or disease.**

Which of the following reactions of the citric acid cycle forms CO_2 as one of its products?

    (A)   Succinate to fumarate

    (B)   Isocitrate to α-ketoglutarate

    (C)   Phosphoenolpyruvate to pyruvate

    (D)   Fructose 1,6-diphosphate to glyceraldehyde 3-phosphate

    (E)   Isocitrate to citrate

Discussion:

The citric acid cycle plays several roles in metabolism through the oxidation of acetyl CoA, which is derived from amino acids, fatty acids, and carbohydrates, to CO_2 and H_2O. Some of the energy released by this exothermic oxidative reaction is stored in the energy-rich bonds of ATP. During this process of oxidative phosphorylation, important by-products such as CO_2 and H_2O are produced at specific stages. When isocitrate is converted to α-keotglutarate, CO_2 is produced. Answer: **B**.

    •   **Biochemistry questions may require calculations.**

An enzyme which obeys simple Michaelis-Menton kinetics has a K_m of 50 mmol/liter and a V_{max} of 210 mmoles/min/mg. The substrate concentration is 5 mmoles/liter. Find the velocity (Vo).

    (A)   31 mmoles/min/mg

    (B)   40 mmoles/min/mg

    (C)   19 mmoles/min/mg

    (D)   25 mmoles/min/mg

    (E)   2 mmoles/min/mg

Discussion:

This question requires that you claculate the velocity of an enzymatic reaction (Vo) using the Michaelis-Menton equation (Vo=V_{max}[S]/K_m+[S]. In this problem, Vo = 210 [5]/50 + 5 = 19 mmol/min/mg. It is important to pay careful attention to units. Answer C.

    •   **Biochemistry questions require that you understand the biochemical basis of disease and may refer to clinical manifestations.**

A 3-year-old boy is brought to your office by his mother for an initial patient visit. The boy is hyperactive and is not yet walking or talking. On examination, you notice that the child has a tremor, is pale, and has blue eyes and blond hair. The patient's mother, a recent immigrant, can not recall his being screened for any genetic diseases at birth. Further cognitive evaluation reveal an estimated IQ of 40. Which of the following enzymatic deficiencies is most likely?

    (A)   Homogentisate oxidase
    (B)   Cystathionine synthetase
    (C)   Glutamine synthetase
    (D)   Glycogen phosphorylase
    (E)   Phenylalanine hydroxylase

Discussion:

This clinical vignette describes symptoms typical of untreated phenylketonuria (PKU), a disease caused by a deficiency in the enzyme pheylalanine hydroxylase, which converts phenylalanine to tyrosine, which is an important precursor for some neurotransmitters. Special diets, low in phenylalanine and high in tyrosine can avoid the symptoms described. Many states require neonatal PKU screening. Answer: **E.**

- **Biochemistry questions require that you use your knowledge of biochemical pathways to predict clinical manifestations of dieases.**

A father brings his daughter to your office because he is concerned that she is eating paint chips that are flaking from the woodwork. Which of the following substances would be elevated in the patient's urine if she had lead poisoning?

    (A)   Coproporphyrin III and B-aminolevulinic acid
    (B)   Heme and porphobilinogen
    (C)   Heme
    (D)   Porphobilinogen
    (E)   Preuroporphyrinogen and uroporphyrin I

Discussion:

Unfortunately, lead poisoning is a common problem due to the prevalence of lead in old paint. After ingestion, lead inhibits a number of enzymes, particularly those involved in heme synthesis. More specifically, the inhibition of the enzymes ferrochelatase and ALA dehydrase leads to the accumulation of coproporphyrin III and d–aminolevulinic acid in urine. Answer: **A.**

Notes

CHAPTER 9

STRATEGIES FOR STUDYING CELL BIOLOGY AND IMMUNOLOGY

Cell Biology is the study of the internal cellular organelles, the extracellular matrix, and their involvement in metabolic processes at the cellular level. Recent scientific advances have led to a much greater understanding of cellular structure and function. A key to success is to relate new information to material learned previously in undergraduate courses, or in other medical school courses, such as Microscopic Anatomy and Biochemistry. **Immunology** is the study of various mechanisms the human body uses to protect from infection due to bacteria, viruses, fungi, and parasites. You will learn about the entire human immune system, both the cellular (cell-mediated) and noncellular (antibody mediated or humoral) components. A key to success is to consider the immune system in context. It is the body's logical response to pathogens you will learn about in Microbiology.

Chapter Overview

A. Develop a good understanding of the general properties of important cells, proteins, and signaling molecules.

B. First, learn characteristics common to all members of a group and then learn the distinguishing features of subgroups.

C. Use illustrations and diagrams to aid in developing conceptualization of the material.

D. Use mnemonics to aid recall.

E. Become familiar with the types of examination questions you will be asked.

A.   Develop a good understanding of the general properties of important cells, proteins, and signaling molecules.

It is helpful to learn general properties before beginning more detailed study of Cell Biology or Immunology. When approaching the immune system, it is useful to recognize that the cell-mediated and *humoral* components both involve a three-step process:

(1) recognition of the foreign object (antigen recognition)

(2) activation of the particular immune components necessary to form a specific response

(3) production of the response and eventual elimination of the antigen.

All of the various components of the immune system are going to function in at least one of these roles and will also communicate with components that function in the others. For example, in the *cell-mediated* component, this 3-step process is

(1) ingestion of an invading bacterium (antigen) by a macrophage cell and display of digested particles on its surface

(2) binding of an antigen specific T-cell to the macrophage with subsequent production of chemical mediators and

(3) clonal proliferation of activated T-cells that fight against bacterial growth.

B.   First, learn characteristics common to all members of a group and then learn the distinguishing features of sub-groups.

Learning the characteristics common to all members of a group will allow you to apply that information to each of its members and will reduce the amount of information you will need to memorize. For example, learning that all T-lymphocytes (a type of cell active in cell-mediated immunity) mature in the *thymus* gland (therefore *T*-lymphocytes) and have the protein CD3 on their surface (CD3+), will enable you to attribute these features to a specific type of T-lymphocyte (helper T-lymphocytes or cytotoxic T-lymphocytes). Likewise, learning that all antibodies (immunoglobulins) are made up of combinations of light and heavy chains will help you understand their common properties of antigen binding, antibody diversity, and gene rearrangement.

C.   Use illustrations, charts, and diagrams to aid in developing conceptualization of the material.

Flowcharts and diagrams concisely capture essential relationships and can aid in making information more meaningful. This strategy is particularly useful when trying to understand the interactions between different classes of cells. **Figure 9.1** will be helpful

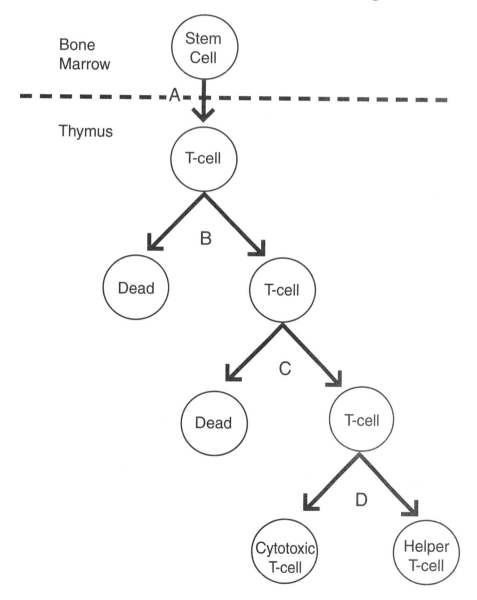

Figure 9.1 T-lymphocyte (T-cell) Development. Adapted from: Levinson, W., M.D., Ph.D. & Jawetz, E., M.D., Ph.D. (2000). *Medical Microbiology & Immunology Examination and Board Review*, p. 347.

when trying to understand the concepts of positive and negative selection in the development of T-lymphocytes (T-cells). These processes begin after the differentiation of stem cells into T-cells (A) and are essential in normal immune function and the maturation and development of T-cells. The process of positive selection (B) allows for the continued survival of the cells that respond appropriately (i.e., exhibit a positive response) when introduced to the body's antigen presenting proteins. Surviving cells then undergo the process of negative selection (C) to eliminate those cells that react with body proteins too strongly. At both stages, the failure to react appropriately results in cell death, leading to T-cells (D) that react with foreign antigens but have "self tolerance" and will not react inappropriately (thus avoiding autoimmune disease).

The chart shown in **Figure 9.2** will be useful when learning the properties and functions of the main classes of antibodies (immunoglobulins.)

Antibody Class	Structure	Percentage of total in serum	Unique Properties	Function
IgG	Two light (L) and two heavy (H) chains (One H2L2 unit)	75%	Crosses placenta Activates complement system Produced by fetus	Main antibody produced in the secondary response
IgA	Two H2L2 units plus one joining (J) chain May also contain a "secretory component"	15%	Present in saliva, tears, breast milk, mucus, etc.	Prevents bacterial and viral invasion of mucus membranes
IgM	Five H2L2 units plus one J chain	9%	Highest binding avidity Activates complement system	Main antibody produced in the primary response
IgE	One H2L2 unit	<1%	Causes release of mediators from mast cells and basophils	Main defense against parasitic infections Main antibody produced in immediate hypersensitivity (allergic response)

Figure 9.2. Properties and Functions of Antibodies

D.   Use mnemonics to aid recall.

Mnemonics may be useful to help you remember. For example, the "rule of eights" can be used to remember the complex interactions between the receptors on the outside of T-lymphocytes and the major histocompatibility complex (MHC) proteins present on macrophages (a different type of immune cell) that display antigens for the T-lymphocytes. Surface receptors on helper T-lymphocytes (those that express the protein CD4, but lack the protein CD8) interact solely with class II MHC proteins (4x2=8). Surface receptors on cytotoxic T-cells (express the protein CD8, but lack the protein CD4) interact solely with class I MHC proteins (8x1=8).

E.   Become familiar with the types of examination questions you will be asked.

- **Cell biology questions require that you understand subcellular organelles and the extracellular matrix.**

Pemphigus vulgaris is a rare disease in which potentially fatal blisters form because of the loss of normal intercellular attachments between the epidermis and dermis and/or muscosal epithelia and lamina propria. It has been shown that people with this condition mount an abnormal immune response against transmembrane glycoproteins leading to the disruption of desmosome function and the loss of skin integrity. Which of the following statements regarding the nature of desmosomes is true?

- (A)   They are located in the basal region of cells, binding them to the basal lamina.
- (B)   They are found solely in epithelial and mucosal cells.
- (C)   They bind to many types of intermediate filaments including keratin, vimentin, and desmin.
- (D)   They are composed of glycosaminoglycans (GAGs), proteins, and other polysaccharides.
- (E)   They facilitate the process of cell coupling by modulating intracellular calcium and cyclic AMP (cAMP) levels.

Discussion:

Desmosomes are found in a wide variety of cell types and bind to intermediate filaments and anchor them in place. However, the specific type of filament to which they bind depends on the cell type and includes keratin (epithelial cells), vimentin (brain cells), and desmin (cardiac muscle cells). Answer: **C**.

- **Cell biology questions require that you understand normal cellular processes.**

Which of the following statements regarding DNA synthesis and repair is correct?

(A) Mitosis halves the number of chromosomes and leads to the formation of sperm and ova.

(B) All DNA is synthesized in the 3' to 5' direction.

(C) During prophase, the nuclear membrane disappears, two copies of each chromosome are arranged at the midpoint of the cell, and the chromosomes attach to the spindle microtubules.

(D) The differences between DNA replication in bacteria (such as *E. coli*) and in humans have little clinical significance.

(E) The synthesis of both the leading and lagging (Okazaki fragments) strand of DNA begins with an RNA primer.

Discussion:

There are no known DNA polymerase enzymes that can initiate the polymerization of a DNA chain. Therefore the synthesis of both the leading strand and the multiple Okazaki fragments in the lagging strand begins with an RNA primer to create a short strand of RNA that is used as an attachment site for DNA polymerase. The segments of RNA are later removed and filled in with appropriate DNA bases. Answer: **E**.

- **Immunology questions require that you understand the basic principles of immunity.**

Which of the following is an example of passive immunity?

(A) Exposure to a bacterial infection.

(B) Exposure to a viral infection.

(C) Administration of a toxoid vaccine.

(D) Administration of a live-attenuated vaccine

(E) Administration of preformed antibodies

Discussion:

Passive immunity is immunity that is gained through antibodies made in another host. Examples of passive immunity include direct inoculation of antibody to neutralize toxins (as in tetanus exposure), the antibody (IgG) passed from mother to fetus during pregnancy, and the antibody (IgA) present in breast milk. The answer choices A, B, C & D are all examples of active immunity. Answer: **E**.

Individuals of blood type O(Rh-)

(A)   Are "universal recipients" of blood transfusions.

(B)   Are "universal donors" of blood transfusions.

(C)   Do not have circulating anti-A or anti-B antibody.

(D)   Have both the A antigen and the B antigen on their red blood cells.

(E)   Have both the A antigen and the B antigen, but they do not cross react.

Discussion:

Patients with type O blood are considered to be "universal donors" because they lack the expression of either the A or B antigens on their cell surface. Therefore, patients in all four blood type groups (Type A, B, AB, or O) can accept transfusions. Patients with blood type AB are considered the "universal recipients" because they lack both anti-A and anti-B antibody, and will not mount an immune response to the transfused blood. Answer: **B**.

- **Immunology questions require that you understand the humoral (antibody-mediated) immune process.**

Which of the following statements regarding the structure or function of antibodies is true?

(A)   The majority of circulating antibody is of IgD type

(B)   Following exposure to an antigen, the first antibodies produced are IgG which are later replaced by IgM.

(C)   IgA is the antibody made in greatest amount by the fetus.

(D)   IgE is the antibody responsible for triggering allergic responses of the anaphylactic (immediate) type.

(E)   Antibodies are the body's main response to viral disease.

Discussion:

Immunoglobulin E (IgE) mediates anaphylactic (immediate) hypersensitivity reactions and is active in host defenses against parasitic infections. In the body, it is found largely bound to mast cells and basophils where it serves as allergen receptors. When an allergen is introduced, IgE mediates the release of pharmacologically active mediators such as histamine, serotonin, leukotrines, and prostaglandins by the mast cells and basophils. Answer: **D**.

- **Immunology questions require that you understand the function of various cell lines in the immune response.**

A 29-year-old male comes to your office with a fever of several weeks duration, fatigue, and a 25-lb weight loss over several weeks. He has noticed "funny white spots" on his tongue and throat that have been worsening despite using mouthwash. He has had severe nausea, vomiting, and diarrhea. You note he is weak and very thin with diffuse lymphadenopathy and oral thrush. Initial blood work shows severe lymphopenia. More extensive blood analysis, including PCR, indicates that the patient is HIV+ and has AIDS. Which of the following best explains this patient's underlying disease?

(A) Loss of helper T-cells (CD4+).

(B) Loss of cytotoxic T-cells (CD8+).

(C) Loss of natural killer cells.

(D) Improper antibody response.

(E) Decreased phagocytic activity by macrophages.

Discussion:

Acquired immunodeficiency syndrome (AIDS) is a severe state of immunosuppression caused by infection with the Human Immunodeficiency Virus (HIV), a retrovirus. This virus causes a disruption of the body's cellular immune response by selectively destroying helper T-cells (CD4+ cells). These cells normally participate in antigen recognition, help B cells develop into antibody producing plasma cells, and help activate cytotoxic T-cells. Without proper helper T-cell response, the body is unable to fight fungal, bacterial, viral, or protozoal opportunistic infections. The body is also more susceptible to neoplasms such as Kaposi sarcoma, lymphoma, and cervical cancer. Answer: **A**.

CHAPTER 10

STRATEGIES FOR STUDYING CLINICAL PATHOPHYSIOLOGY

Clinical Pathophysiology, commonly referred to as "Medicine," involves learning about the manifestation of diseases in specific organ systems. It is often taught in units, e.g., hematology, cardiology, gastroenterology, nephrology, pulmonology, infectious disease, rheumatology, and endocrinology. It serves as a summative, "capstone" course that helps make the transition from the basic science years to the clinical years. In this course you will examine individual and constellations of physical signs and symptoms to provide the basis for a list of differential diagnoses, and ultimately, the one diagnosis that best explains them. Mastering this subject requires incorporating information learned in basic science courses with clinical problem solving skills. Most students enjoy learning to formulate diagnoses and develop treatment plans—significant steps to becoming a physician.

Chapter Overview

A. Utilize knowledge from previous basic science courses, especially Anatomy, Physiology, and Pathology.

B. Pay close attention to terminology.

C. First learn typical presentations, then learn atypical ones

D. Use charts and diagrams to consolidate and organize information and to aid in developing conceptualization of the material.

E. Approach presenting problems consistently and systematically.

F. Become familiar with the types of examination questions you will be asked.

105

A.   Utilize knowledge from previous basic science courses, especially Anatomy, Physiology and Pathology.

Much of the material presented in your Clinical Pathophysiology course will require the utilization and integration of knowledge learned in courses already completed, such as Anatomy, Physiology, and Pathology. Therefore, a key to success is to begin the study of a particular system with a review of the relevant material covered in these courses. By first reviewing the normal structure and function of an organ system, you will better understand the pathophysiology involved with disease of that system.

For example, when studying the cardiovascular system, begin first by reviewing the normal anatomy, blood pressure regulatory systems, cardiac cycle (including the heart sounds, phases of contraction/relaxation and pressure-volume relationships), and pathologic findings in common diseases (atherosclerosis, ischemic heart disease, congestive heart failure, etc.). When studying the renal system, begin by first reviewing the normal kidney structure, acidosis/alkalosis and other physiological processes (glomerular filtration, nephron and collecting tubule excretion/reabsorbtion, and hormonal activity), and the pathologic findings in common diseases (renal failure, kidney stones, electrolyte disturbances, etc.).

B.   Pay close attention to terminology.

Much of the terminology used in the study of Clinical Pathophysiology is historically derived and must be memorized. Physical findings, diseases, and syndromes may be named after people (Rovsing sign, Alzheimer disease, Paget disease, Down syndrome), places (Lyme disease, Rocky Mountain spotted fever, Norweigan scabies), mythology (*caput medusae*), or may be borrowed from other languages (*peau d'orange* and *café au lait* spots). However, careful attention and reasoning can be helpful in remembering these terms. For example, the tortuous venous pattern seen around the umbilicus (belly button) in patients with portal hypertension is said to resemble Medusa's (a Greek mythological figure) hair of snakes, and is described with the term *caput medusae*. The inflammatory reaction seen with some types of breast cancer can make the skin overlying the tumor look like an orange peel, thus described with the French term *peau d'orange*.

C. First learn typical presentations, then learn atypical ones.

A common saying that you are likely to hear during medical school is: "If you hear hoof steps in the distance, it is most likely horses, not zebras." In other words, common diseases occur commonly. Therefore, when thinking about all of the possible etiologies of patients' complaints, the most likely diagnoses will be those that are the most common. For example, when diagnosing a healthy 24-year-old male with a cough, a diagnosis of an allergy, viral or bacterial illness is much more likely than a diagnosis of congestive heart failure (because allergies, viral and bacterial illnesses are much more common in this age group than is heart failure.) When determining the underlying cause of a patient's complaints and developing a diagnosis, keep in mind, common diseases occur commonly.

Diseases also often become clinically "noticed" (i.e., they present) because of their most common symptoms. Therefore, when trying to remember the specifics of a disease, it is helpful to focus on understanding the most common symptoms first. For example, first learn the common presentation of rheumatoid arthritis: symmetrical, bilateral pain and morning stiffness of the wrist, metacarpal phalangeal, and proximal interphalangeal joints, with relative sparing of the distal interphalangeal joints. Then learn details regarding blood findings, and x-ray changes. Eventually you will learn the less common symptoms, such as extra-articular involvement (heart, lung, nerve, eye and vision problems), as patients do complain of these less common symptoms as well.

D. Use illustrations, charts, and diagrams to consolidate and organize information and to aid in developing conceptualization of the material.

Charts and tables can concisely capture essential relationships and are effective tools to identify and remember distinctions between similar diseases. An illustration of this can be seen in **Figure 10.1** as Crohn disease and ulcerative colitis are two of the most common inflammatory bowel diseases. Although they are both characterized by inflammation and damage to the gastrointestinal tract and have many similar complications and extra-intestinal manifestations, each has important distinctions (as illustrated here.)

CHARACTERISTICS	CROHN DISEASE	ULCERATIVE COLITIS
Location	Any portion of the GI tract, but most common in terminal ileum	Only rectum with variable involvement of colon
Lesion morphology	"Skip lesions" with transmural inflammation	"Continuous lesions" with inflammation limited to mucosa and submucosa
Gross appearance (Colonoscopic findings)	"Cobblestone" mucosa with ulcers and fissures "Creeping" fat	Red granular mucosa Friable pseudopolyps Bowel wall edema
Microscopic appearance	Noncaseating granulomas Lymphocytic infiltrate	Crypt abcesses Mucosal ulcers
Radiologic appearance	"String sign" on x-ray Transverse fissures and ulcers on barium enema	"Lead pipe" appearance on barium enema
Complications	Intestinal stricture and fistula formation Malabsorption syndrome Small increase in colorectal carcinoma	Colonic perforation Intestinal bleeding Chronic diarrhea Marked increase in colorectal carcinoma
Treatment	Surgery may be necessary, but is not curative	Surgery may be curative

Figure 10.1. Inflammatory Bowel Disease: A Comparison of Crohn Disease and Ulcerative Colitis

E.   Approach presenting problems consistently and systematically.

Clinical Pathophysiology is often taught as a system-based course by organ system units. However, you will often be required to consider multiple etiologies across multiple organ systems when addressing patient concerns and creating a differential diagnosis. Approaching problems consistently and systematically will insure accuracy.

Consider a 34-year-old female who presents to the emergency room complaining of right-sided upper abdominal pain. There are many possible causes for this patient's pain: perforated ulcer, gallstones, kidney stones, an inferior heart attack, gastritis, hepatitis, pneumonia, a pulmonary embolus, a benign or malignant tumor, appendicitis, or pancreatitis.

If you approach presenting problems consistently and systematically, you will decrease the chance of missing a possible diagnosis. We might approach this patient by thinking about possible diagnoses in order of decreasing severity. In this case we would first consider *acute*, sudden, causes of abdominal pain (gallstones, appendicitis, perforated ulcer, heart disease, hepatitis, pneumonia, gastritis, and other infections.) Then, we would consider *chronic* causes of her pain (masses, tumors, indolent infections.) However, instead, we might approach this patient by thinking of a possible diagnosis from an *anatomic standpoint*. In this approach we might first consider gall bladder disease (gallstones, infection), then liver disease (hepatitis, infection, liver tumors), kidney disease (kidney stones, infection), gastric disease (gastritis, perforated ulcer), pulmonary disease (pneumonia, pulmonary embolus), and cardiac disease (inferior heart attack, pericarditis).

Now, consider a 60-year-old male complaining of acute left-sided chest pain. As with the patient above, you might approach his diagnosis by first considering the immediately life-threatening causes of chest pain: coronary artery and ischemic heart disease, aortic dissection, pneumothorax, and pulmonary embolism. Later, you might want to consider other causes of acute chest pain: benign and malignant tumors, arthritis/costochondritis, musculoskeletal injury, depression and anxiety. If you were to approach this patient from an anatomic standpoint, you would first consider cardiac causes and then vascular, pulmonary, gastrointestinal, musculoskeletal, infectious, and psychiatric causes.

F. Become familiar with the types of examination questions you will be asked.

- **Clinical pathophysiology questions may require that you understand physical signs and symptoms:**

Which of the following statements best characterizes the physical findings noted in mitral valve stenosis?

(A)   A systolic ejection murmur.

(B)   Increased intensity of S1 and the P2 component of S2.

(C)   A holosystolic apical murmur that radiates to the axilla and is accompanied by a thrill.

(D)   Nonspecific changes in all EKG leads.

(E)   A pericardial friction rub heard during both systole and diastole.

Discussion:

Mitral valve stenosis (stiffening of the mitral valve), commonly seen secondary to rheumatic heart disease, impedes left ventricular filling, produces pulmonary congestion, and can lead to decreased cardiac output and right heart failure. Symptoms often include signs of left heart failure (dyspnea, orthopnea, and paroxysmal nocturnal dyspnea) and/or right heart failure (edema, ascites, and fatigue). It can lead to changes in the normal heart sounds including increased intensity of S1 and the P2 component of S2, opening snap following S2, and a diastolic rumble. Common findings on physical exam include atrial fibrillation (irregular heart beat), pulmonary rales (due to fluid in the lungs), and findings of right heart failure (distended neck veins, edema, ascites.) Choice C is often seen in mitral valve regurgitation. Answer: **B**.

• **Clinical pathophysiology questions require that you make diagnoses.**

A 25-year-old male comes to your office complaining of easy bruising, frequent nosebleeds, and gingival bleeding exacerbated by aspirin. He also makes vague mention of a family history of bleeding. Physical examination is normal. You obtain blood work that shows the following results:

Patient Results		Normal Values
Platelet count:	300,000	150-400,000/ul
Bleeding Time:	12 min	2-7.5 min
PTT:	45 sec	11-14 sec
PT:	14 sec	12-20 sec

What is the most likely diagnosis?

    (A)   Thrombocytopenia

    (B)   Hemophilia A (Factor VIII deficiency)

    (C)   Hemophilia B (Factor IX deficiency)

    (D)   Von Willebrand disease (vWF deficiency)

    (E)   Disseminated intravascular coagulation (DIC)

Discussion:

This patient has a prolonged bleeding time and activated partial thromboplastin time (PTT) with a normal platelet count and prothrombin time (PT). Von Willebrand disease (an autosomal dominant disease) leads to decreased amounts of von Willebrand factor (vWF) and metabolically active factor VIII. Because factor VIII is an essential intermediary in the intrinsic coagulation pathway (measured by the PTT), we see a prolongation in the PTT. vWF is necessary for normal platelet function and a deficiency results in a prolonged bleeding time. Because other factors, or the platelets themselves, are not affected, there is no impact on the extrinsic coagulation pathway (the PT is normal) or the platelet count. Answer: **D.**

- **Clinical pathophysiology questions require the interpretation of diagnostic tests.**

On an upper gastrointestinal series, which of the following findings would be most indicative of a malignant gastric ulcer?

    (A)   A thickened, nondistensible stomach (*linitis plastica*)

    (B)   Ulcer crater extending beyond the gastric wall.

    (C)   Gastic folds radiating into the base of the ulcer.

    (D)   Thick radiolucent collar of edema surrounding the ulcer base.

    (E)   Smooth, round or ovoid ulcer crater.

Discussion:

Gastric cancer typically presents with weight loss, anorexia, and epigastric pain, although it may be asymptomatic until the cancer is quite advanced. Typical findings on upper gastrointestinal series include a mass, ulcer, or a diffusely thickened, non-distensible stomach, termed *linitis plastica*. Definitive diagnosis can often be made by endoscopy with biopsy and cytology. Choices B, C, D and E are all radiographic criteria for benign gastric ulcers. Answer: **A.**

- **Clinical pathophysiology questions require knowledge of preventative and therapeutic modalities.**

A 62-year-old, previously healthy male, is hospitalized because of severe shortness of breath, generalized weakness, a fever of 102.5° F., shaking chills, and a cough productive of "rust-colored" sputum. He has not been able to tolerate food or water intake. Initial Gram staining shows multiple Gram-positive cocci in pairs. Which of the following treatments is most appropriate?

- (A)   Supportive therapy only (antibiotics are not indicated)

- (B)   Metronidazole

- (C)   Penicillin

- (D)   Ciprofloxacin

- (E)   Rifampin

Discussion:

The clinical scenario and Gram stain findings are consistent with a diagnosis of community acquired pneumococcal pneumonia. In this case, penicillin is the drug of choice, although erythromycin can be used in penicillin-allergic patients. Because of the severity of the illness, hospitalization is warranted. Answer: **C**.

- **Clinical pathophysiology questions require knowledge of syndromes associated with certain conditions.**

After presenting with signs and symptoms of hyperaldosteronism, a female patient of yours was recently diagnosed with a unilateral small adrenal adenoma and underwent surgery after a failure of spironolactone to control her symptoms. Based on your understanding of this condition, which set of findings did she most likely exhibit?

- (A)   Central obesity, hypertension, decreased glucose tolerance, purple striae, muscular wasting, and hirsutism.

- (B)   Hyperpigmentation, hypotension, hypoglycemia, anorexia, nausea, vomiting, lethargy, and confusion.

- (C)   Paroxysmal hypertension with postural hypotension, headache, sweating, palpitation, weight loss, and tremor.

- (D)   Amenorrhea, acne, hirsutism, and obesity

- (E)   Elevated blood pressure, muscle weakness, and paresthesias.

Discussion:

Excessive production of aldosterone, accompanied by failure of the normal feedback-inhibition pathway, can lead to the increased reabsorption of sodium and excretion of potassium and hydrogen in the distal renal tubules. This results in elevated blood pressure (secondary to sodium retention) and hypokalemia (secondary to potassium loss) that can lead to muscle weakness, paresthesias, and tetany. Spironolactone, an aldosterone antagonist, is often effective in correcting the hypertension and hypokalemia. If unsuccessful, surgical removal is often curative. Choice A is seen in Cushing syndrome (excessive production of cortisol). Choice B is seen in Addison disease (adrenal insufficiency). Choice C is typical of pheochromocytoma, a tumor of chromaffin cells. Choice D is seen in polycystic ovary syndrome. Answer: **E.**

Notes

CHAPTER 11

STRATEGIES FOR STUDYING EPIDEMIOLOGY AND BIOSTATISTICS

Epidemiology involves learning about the incidence and prevalence of diseases within a population. Its primary focus is on the design of studies, the collection and analysis of data, the interpretation of findings, and the development and maintenance of public health and disease surveillance systems. **Biostatistics** involves developing and applying the statistical techniques and theory necessary to design research studies and evaluate medical data. Together, these important courses will improve your ability to understand research methodology and to evaluate scientific papers. A key to success is to set aside any anxiety you might have about mathematics and statistics and to first think conceptually in clinical terms, rather than focusing on the numbers.

Chapter Overview

A. Become familiar with the basics and build from there.

B. Learn terminology in a meaningful way.

C. Use templates to aid in calculations.

D. Practice, practice, practice. Become comfortable with the calculations required.

E. Become familiar with the types of examination questions you will be asked.

A.   Become familiar with the basics and build from there.

To master Epidemiology and Biostatistics, you must become familiar with their basic building blocks. In Epidemiology, these include identifying different types of study designs (cohort vs. case control, retrospective vs. prospective, etc.) and performing basic calculations (sensitivity, specificity, relative risk, etc.). When these are mastered, calculating confidence intervals and displaying and interpreting the medical relevance of results becomes possible.

In Biostatistics, you must become familiar with various types of data (e.g., binary vs. continuous variables), perform basic calculations (range, mean, mode, median, standard deviation), describe statistical distributions (normal, bimodal, positive, negative), and understand the significance of a Type I (α-error) and a Type II error (β-error). This knowledge is basic to computing and understanding z- and t-values, analysis of variance (ANOVA), and survival analysis.

B.   Learn terminology in a meaningful way.

Students often have difficulty with Epidemiology and Biostatistics because they are not familiar with specific terms and their application. Each term has a specific definition that predicts its use. Here are three examples:

Prevalence and Incidence: *Prevalence* refers to how common a particular disease is, i.e., the total number of cases in a population at a given time. The term *incidence* refers to the rate at which new cases develop, i.e., the number of new cases in a given time period. When these terms are understood, it is clear that for chronic ("long-term") diseases, the prevalence will be higher than the incidence (for each time period more new cases are added to the total number of cases.) For acute ("short-term") diseases, the prevalence and incidence will be approximately equal (cases resolve as soon as others are added).

Sensitivity and Specificity: When determining the usefulness of screening and diagnostic tests, *sensitivity* is defined as the number of positive test results divided by the true number of disease cases. *Specificity* is defined as the number of negative test results divided by the true number of those without the disease. To help in understanding this, consider an example of a fishing boat looking for tuna: If the fisherman uses a very sensitive method (such as a very large net) he will likely gather most of the available tuna, but he will also catch many other undesirable fish (false positives). However, if the fisherman uses a very specific method (such as a single lure that only attracts tuna), he will limit his catch to tuna, but will gather many fewer of the potentially available tuna. Thus, screening tests have high sensitivity, to identify as many potential cases as possible, and diagnostic tests have high specificity, to limit the false positive rate.

Accuracy and Precision: When considering the *accuracy* and *precision* of a test, it is useful to think of shooting at a target. The *accuracy* of a test refers to the degree that the test results reflect reality, i.e., a measure of how close each individual shot comes to the bull's-eye. The *precision* of a test refers to the degree that a test reproduces results over several trials, i.e. how close each shot is to the prior shots regardless of where they are on the target. For example, a blood pressure cuff is considered accurate if it correctly measures blood pressure (compared to an invasive test), and precise if it measures the same pressure over several attempts.

C.   Use templates to aid in calculations.

Templates help summarize and organize information contained in passages and help simplify calculations.

Example 1: This template can be used to facilitate your calculations when dealing with **case control** and **cohort studies**.

	EXPOSURE	
OUTCOME (DISEASE)	Yes	No
Yes	(a)	(b)
No	(c)	(d)

Case control studies are used to generate an Odds Ratio (OR)

OR = (a) (d) / (b) (c)

Cohort studies are used to generate Relative Risk (RR)

RR = [a/a+b] / [c/c+d]

Example 2: There are many useful descriptive statistics to evaluate the utility of a clinical test. This template can be used to facilitate your calculations.

	TRUE DISEASE STATUS	
TEST RESULT	Yes	No
Positive	(a)	(b)
Negative	(c)	(d)

Sensitivity	(a) / (a) + (c)
False negative rate	1 – sensitivity
Specificity	(d) / (b) + (d)
False positive rate	1 – specificity
Positive predictive value	(a) / (a) + (b)
Negative predictive value	(d) / (c) + (d)

D. Practice, practice, practice. Become comfortable with the calculations required.

The best way to become comfortable with problem solving in Epidemiology and Biostatistics is to do a variety of sample calculations and problems. You will need to read passages, set up tables, perform calculations and interpret the results in a manner relevant to the clinical problem. The following is a case control study:

You are a researcher interested in the association between prenatal maternal alcohol use and low-birth-weight infants. To evaluate this relationship, you design a case control study involving 200 women who recently gave birth: 100 mothers of low-birth-weight babies and 100 mothers of normal-birth-weight babies were questioned about their use of alcohol during pregnancy. Initial results show 36 mothers of low-birth-weight infants and 5 mothers of normal-weight infants admitted to using alcohol during pregnancy. Determine the odds ratio associated with maternal alcohol use and low-birth-weight infants and interpret the results.

To figure this out, first organize the data into a table as follows:

OUTCOME	EXPOSURE	
	Maternal alcohol use	No maternal alcohol use
Low-birth weight	36 (a)	64 (b)
Normal-birth weight	5 (c)	95 (d)

Then, plug the numbers into the odds ratio formula (because the passage describes a case control study), as described in Example 1 in Section C above:

$$OR = (a)\ (d)\ /\ (b)\ (c)$$

$$OR = (36)\ (95)\ /\ (64)\ (5) = 3420\ /\ 320 = 10.7$$

Interpretation of results:

In the population studied, an infant born to a mother who used alcohol during her pregnancy is 10.7 times more likely to be of low-birth weight as compared to an infant whose mother did not drink alcohol.

E. Become familiar with the types of examination questions you will be asked.

- **Biostatistics questions require that you calculate values.**

You are conducting a cross-sectional study of the relationship between heart disease and smoking among 1000 randomly selected people (500 are smokers and 500 are nonsmokers.) You obtain the following results:

	Heart disease	
	Present	Absent
Smokers	300	200
Nonsmokers	100	400

What is the prevalence of heart disease in this population?

    (A) 20%

    (B) 30%

    (C) 35%

    (D) 40%

    (E) 50%

Discussion:

Prevalence is defined as the total number of cases in the total population at a given time. In this study, 400 out of the total study population of 1000 have heart disease, or 40%. As a reminder, incidence is defined as the number of new cases in a given time period. Because this question describes a cross-sectional study, the time period is not available and the incidence rate can not be calculated from the given information. Answer: **D**.

- **Biostatistics questions require that you interpret results.**

In conducting research on lung cancer, you develop a large prospective cohort study comparing people with significant asbestos exposure to people without known exposure. Your initial results show that the relative risk of developing lung cancer for those exposed is 14. This implies that:

  (A)   14% of all lung cancer patients were exposed to asbestos.

  (B)   The incidence of lung cancer in patients with known asbestos exposure is 14 times greater than the non-exposed.

  (C)   The prevalence of lung cancer among those exposed to asbestos is 14 times that among non-smokers.

  (D)   14% of all people exposed to asbestos develop lung cancer

  (E)   14% of people develop lung cancer

Discussion:

Relative risk, which can be derived from cohort studies, is defined as the risk of disease in the exposed group divided by the risk in the non-exposed group. It is a statement of the increased likelihood of disease as a result of the exposure. Answer: **B**.

- **Epidemiology questions require that you understand study design.**

A researcher is interested in conducting a study examining the relationship between maternal exposure to environmental risk factors and the development of a rare childhood metabolic disease. In setting up the study, which design is most appropriate?

(A) Case control

(B) Prospective cohort

(C) Double-blinded, placebo-controlled clinical trial

(D) Retrospectice cohort

(E) Cross-sectional

Discussion:

In case control studies, samples are first chosen base on the presence (case) or absence (control) of disease. Later, information is collected about risk factors and exposures. This type of study is well suited for investigating rare disease. Answer: **A**.

- **Epidemiology questions may require that you understand the basic tenants of public health.**

A 56-year-old male presents to the local emergency room with complaints of severe chest pain and acute changes on his EKG suggestive of an acute myocardial infarction ("heart attack"). After being seen by the *cardiologist on-call*, it is recommended that the patient undergo immediate cardiac catheterization. This is an example of:

(A) Primary prevention

(B) Secondary prevention

(C) Tertiary prevention

(D) Unnecessary treatment

Discussion:

Tertiary prevention aims to prevent additional damage and reduce disability from an existing disease (in this case further damage to the heart following the heart attack). Primary prevention is aimed at preventing disease occurrence (e.g., weight loss and a healthy diet). Secondary prevention is aimed at the early detection of disease (e.g., exercise stress test). Answer: **C**.

Notes

CHAPTER 12

STRATEGIES FOR STUDYING MEDICAL GENETICS

Medical Genetics is the study of chromosomal anomalies, genes, gene products (such as enzymes, transport, or structural proteins), and other inherited characteristics that may be found isolated in individuals or clustered in related families. You will need to understand the basic mechanisms of human heredity (i.e., Mendelian vs. multifactorial vs. sex-linked) and the etiologic role that inherited genes and new mutations play in the development of normal traits and disease syndromes. You will learn how to predict the likelihood that carriers of a gene will have affected offspring. In addition, perhaps you will learn about well-defined clinical syndromes with a genetic basis.

Chapter Overview

A. Become familiar with the basic terminology and notation and build from there.

B. Use illustrations and diagrams, including pedigree construction; summarize information using family trees.

C. Practice, practice, practice. Become familiar with the calculations required.

D. Become familiar with the types of examination questions you will be asked.

A. Become familiar with the basic terminology and notation and build from there.

Like most subjects, medical genetics uses specific terminology. To master genetics, you must learn several unique definitions and terms and become familiar with their use. Some examples are illustrated in **Figure 12.1**. Learning this terminology early in your studying will aid in understanding.

Additionally, you should also become familiar with the symbols used in pedigree construction and analysis. Some of the commonly used symbols are shown in **Figure 12.2**. It will be helpful to refer to this when reading the passage on pages 125 and 126.

TERM	DEFINITION	USAGE/EXAMPLE
Gene	Inherited information that determines an individual's genetic makeup	Humans have thousands of genes that code for thousands of characteristics
Allele	The various possible expressions of the same gene	For a given characteristic (e.g., hair color), various allelic possibilities exist (brown, blond, etc.)
Genotype	The genetic material contained in a given gene at a particular location on one of the human chromosomes	A person with two alleles for brown hair is said to have the genotype for brown hair
Phenotype	The observable expression of a particular gene after the interaction of the genetic information with the environment	If too much time is spent in the sun, a person with the allele for brown hair can phenotypically exhibit blond hair.
Dominant allele	An allele in which only one copy is required to express the phenotype	In autosomal dominant diseases (such as Huntington disease), only one copy of the dominent allele is needed to inherit the disease.
Recessive allele	An allele in which two copies are necessary in order to express the phenotype	In autosomal recessive diseases (such as cystic fibrosis) two copies of the recessive allele must be inherited (one from each parent).
Homozygous	The possession of two copies of the same allele for a given gene	A person with two copies of the allele for blond hair (one copy inherited from each parent) is said to be homozygous for that trait.
Heterozygous	The possession of two different alleles for a given gene	A person with one allele for blond hair and one allele for brown hair is heterozygous for that trait.

Figure 12.1

B. Use illustrations, charts, and diagrams, including pedigree construction; summarize information using family trees.

You learned in Chapter 3: Maintenance that flowcharts and diagrams can often capture essential relationships in a concise way, and can aid in making information more meaningful to you. This strategy is particularly useful when studying genetics and trying to understand the specific pattern of genetic heritability involved. It can be difficult to understand essential relationships when just reading a passage. However, when a family pedigree is used to summarize this information, patterns become easier to identify. Consider the following passage and pedigree:

An adolescent male was recently diagnosed with disease X, which his doctors believe is genetically based. Both of his parents deny ever having symptoms, although they have never undergone any specific genetic testing. The couple has three other children (two girls and one boy) all of whom are

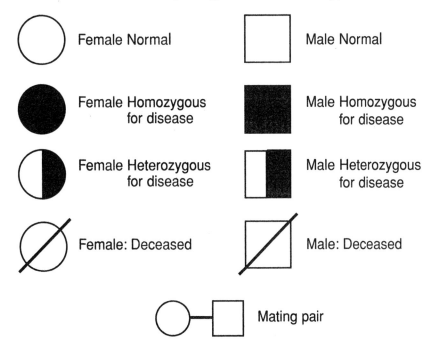

Figure 12.2 Commonly Used Symbols in Pedigree Construction and Analysis

asymptomatic. Additionally, both parents denied a history of the disease in both their immediate and extended families. In working up the possible genetic basis of this disease, both parents are identified as heterozygote for the disease trait, i.e. asymptomatic carriers. Additionally, it is found that one of their daughters and one of their sons are also carriers. The remaining daughter tests negative for the trait as does the patient's brother-in-law and niece. This information is depicted in the following pedigree:

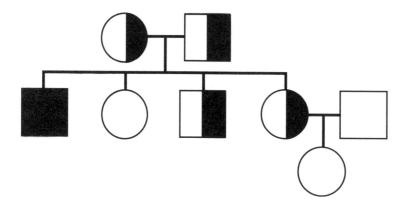

This is a common pattern in *autosomal recessive diseases* (cystic fibrosis, sickle cell anemia, etc.) and most of the inborn errors of metabolism (phenylketonuria, galactosemia, lysosomal storage diseases, etc.)

The study of genetics requires visual differentiation of patients with a variety of disorders. Techniques described in Chapter 6: Microscopic Anatomy will be useful for comparing visual information. Similar genetic syndromes can be distinguished by visible facial or body abnormalities (cleft lip, low-set ears, rocker bottom feet, etc.), or by congenital abnormalities (malformations of internal organs, e.g., heart defects.). It is helpful to select distinguishing features and to summarize information in a table format. In **Figures 12.3** and **12.4**, distinguishing features are highlighted in boldface type.

DISORDERS	ETIOLOGY (most common)	VISIBLE ANOMALIES	INTERNAL ANOMALIES	PROGNOSIS
Patau Syndrome	Trisomy 13 (47, XX +13)	**Cleft lip and palate** **Polydactyly** **Micropthalmia** Umbilical hernia Rocker bottom feet	Mental retardation Cardiac defects Renal defects	Rarely survive beyond 1 year
Edwards Syndrome	Trisomy 18 (47, XX +18)	**Low-set ears** **Overlapping fingers** **Micrognathia** Rocker bottom feet	**Limited hip abduction** Mental retardation Cardiac defects Renal malformations	Rarely survive beyond 1 year
Down Syndrome	Trisomy 21 (47, XX +21)	**Epicanthic folds** **Flat facial profile** **Simian crease** **Sandal-toe gap** Umbilical hernia	**Intestinal stenosis** **Hypotonia** Mental retardation Cardiac defects	**Long-term survival** Increased risk for: Leukemia Infection Alzheimer disease

Figure 12.3. Disorders of Trisomy

DISORDERS	ETIOLOGY (most common)	VISIBLE ANOMALIES	INTERNAL ANOMALIES	PROGNOSIS
Turner Syndrome	(45,X)	**Low posterior hairline** **Webbed neck** **Broad chest** **Lymph-stasis edema** Short stature	**Aortic coarctation** **Streak ovaries** **Primary amenorrhea** Cardiac defects	Long-term survival **Increased risk for:** **Infertility** **Obesity** **Diabetes** **Anti-thyroid ab** **Hypothyroid**
Klinefelter Syndrome	(47,XXY)	**Eunuchoid body** **Long legs** **Few secondary sex characteristics** Gynecomastia	**Atrophic testes** Questionable low IQ	Long-term survival **Increased risk for:** **Infertility**
XYY Syndrome	(47,XYY)	**Severe acne** Tall	Normal intelligence	Long-term survival **Questionable risk of:** **Antisocial behavior** **Impulse-control disorders**

Figure 12.4. Disorders of Sex Chromosomes

C. Practice, practice, practice. Become familiar with the calculations required.

In genetics, calculations may be required to determine the prevalence of a gene in the population, the likelihood that a given individual is a carrier, or to estimate the risk that a child will inherit the gene from his parents. The best way to become comfortable with the calculations is to do a variety of practice problems.

The **Hardy-Weinberg equilibrium** has been developed to aid in calculations, but its use requires a large, randomly mating population and knowledge of the *allelic frequency* (frequency of one allele relative to all the other alleles), the *genotypic frequency* (frequency of people that share a specific genotype), and the *phenotypic frequency* (frequency of people that share a phenotype). These are expressed mathematically as follows:

For a given gene with two alleles A and a:

If the frequency of the A allele = p and the frequency of the a allele = q, then:

The total *allelic frequency* (A allele + a allele) = $p + q = 1$

The *genotypic frequency* = $p^2 + 2pq + q^2 = 1$,

where p^2 = frequency of individuals with genotype AA
$2pq$ = frequency of individuals with genotype Aa
q^2 = frequency of individuals with genotype aa

The Hardy-Weinberg equilibrium also assumes that the "gene pool" is stable and randomly selected, i.e., that there are no new mutations, migration/immigration, or natural selection that favors survival of one of the genotypes at the expense of the other.

The use of these principles is illustrated in the following example:

Wilson disease is a rare autosomal recessive disorder of copper metabolism that leads to the accumulation of toxic levels of copper in many tissues including the eye, liver, and brain. Untreated, it can progress to acute or chronic liver disease, neuropsychiatric changes, or a Parkinson disease-like syndrome and can be fatal. In the general population, it has an incidence of approximately 0.3 per 10,000 live births. The Hardy-Weinberg equilibrium can be used to determine the frequency of carriers in the general population.

A good way to approach this problem is as follows:

1. We are told that the frequency of Wilson disease is .3/10,000. Therefore, $q^2 = 0.00003$ and $q = \sqrt{q^2} = 0.0055$

2. Since p+q = 1, p + (.0055) = 1 and p = 0.9945

3. $2pq = 2 (0.9945) (0.0055) = 0.0109$

In other words, the frequency of carriers (heterozygotes) in the general population is 0.0109 and the frequency of homozygous dominant people in the general population is 0.9945.

D. Become familiar with the types of examination questions you will be asked.

- **Genetics questions require that you interpret pedigree analysis.**

Several members of a family are effected with an unknown disease. Given this family tree, which of the following diseases is most likely?

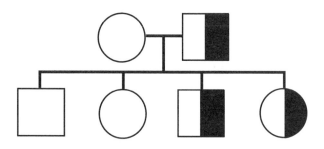

(A) Cystic fibrosis

(B) Von Willebrand disease

(C) Galactosemia

(D) Tay-Sachs disease

(E) Von Gierke disease

Discussion:

The mode of inheritance depicted is that of autosomal dominance. Von Willebrand disease follows an autosomal dominant pattern of inheritance and is the most common hereditary bleeding disorder. It is characterized by a deficiency of von Willebrand factor (vWF), a protein necessary for proper platelet adhesion and hemostasis. All of the other answer choices are transmitted through autosomal recessive inheritance. Answer: **B**.

- Genetics questions require that you understand the specific mechanisms of genetic heritability

Which of the following disorders is due to the chromosomal anomaly known as "deletion"?

    (A)   Fragile X syndrome

    (B)   Neurofibromatosis

    (C)   Prader-Willi syndrome

    (D)   Friedreich ataxia

    (E)   Huntington disease

Discussion:

Prader-Willi syndrome is due to a genetic deletion in the paternally derived chromosome 15 in a process known as "imprinting." Prader-Willi syndrome is characterized by small hands and feet, obesity, short stature, hypotonia, hypogonadism, and mental retardation. A deletion in the maternally derived chromosome 15 results in Angelman syndrome, a clinically distinct entity consisting of ataxic gait, seizures, inappropriate laughter, and mental retardation. Answer: **C**.

- Genetic questions require that you estimate the risk of disease in the offspring.

You are seen in your office by a couple who desires to have a child. The husband has a medical history significant for Hemophilia A (X-linked recessive) and they want to know the risk of having a child with the same disease. The wife is unaffected. Which of the following statements concerning this couple is correct?

    (A)   The gene will be passed to every son, but none of the daughters.

    (B)   The gene will be passed to every daughter, but none of the sons.

    (C)   There is a 50% chance that the gene will be transmitted to each son and each daughter.

    (D)   There is a 50% chance that the gene will be transmitted to each daughter, but all the sons will be unaffected.

    (E)   There is a 50% chance that the gene will be transmitted to each son, but the daughters will be unaffected.

Discussion:

A male with an X-linked recessive allele will pass it to all of his daughters, but to none of his sons. However, a heterogeneous female with an X-linked recessive allele (a carrier) can pass the trait on to both her sons and daughters. If she mates with an unaffected male, there is a 50% chance that she will transmit the gene to her son or daughter. While the sons will exhibit the disease (in this case Hemophilia A), the daughters will likely remain asymptomatic carriers. Answer: **B**.

- **Genetic questions require that you recognize specific genetic syndromes.**

The findings of a low posterior hairline, webbing of the neck, and a broad chest with widely spaced nipples in a 17-year-old female complaining of amenorrhea (lack of menses), is most consistent with which of the following diagnoses?

    (A)   Klinefelter syndrome (47,XXY)

    (B)   XYY syndrome (47,XYY)

    (C)   Turner syndrome (45,X)

    (D)   Hermaphroditism (46,XX)

    (E)   Pseudohermaphroditism (46,XX)

Discussion:

Turner syndrome is the most common sex chromosome abnormality in females. It results from complete or partial monosomy (one copy) of the X chromosome. Classic findings include short stature, low posterior hairline, webbing of the neck, displaced elbows (cubitus valgus), and a broad chest with widely spaced nipples. Other findings may include congenital heart disease, aortic narrowing (coarctation of the aorta), streak ovaries (and therefore infertility and amenorrhea), and multiple moles (pigmented nevi). Affected patients typically present in infancy, but milder forms may go undiagnosed until delayed menses leads to further evaluation. Answer: **C.**

- **Genetic questions require that you know common complications of genetic syndromes.**

When making rounds in the nursery, you notice that one of the newborns has prominent epicanthal folds and a flat facial profile. On further exam, you also notice a simian crease, prominent gap between the first and second toe, and a murmur consistent with an atrial septal defect. Karyotypic analysis confirms the diagnosis of Down syndrome (Trisomy 21). This infant is at additional risk of which of the following?

    (A)   Leukemia

    (B)   Renal malformations

    (C)   Alcoholism

    (D)   Chronic Obstructive Pulmonary Disease(COPD)

    (E)   Atherosclerosis

Discussion:

Down syndrome is characterized by findings of epicanthal folds, flat facial profile, simian crease, "sandal-toe" (gap between first and second toe), and mental retardation. Many affected individuals also have congenital heart disease and other congenital malformations including esophageal atresia. In addition to leukemia, individuals with Down syndrome also have increased risk of developing serious infections, Alzheimer disease, and thyroid autoimmunity. Answer: **A**

CHAPTER 13

STRATEGIES FOR STUDYING MICROBIOLOGY

Microbiology is the study of microorganisms such as bacteria, viruses, fungi, helmiths (worms), and protozoa that cause human disease. Comprehension and retention of information about this wide variety or organisms requires remembering a multitude of details, some of which are specific to one organism, but others that may be characteristic of several different organisms. A key to success is to make these similarities and differences more apparent during study by creating charts that compare and contrast these details and consolidating information. While the approach to bacteriology will be discussed in this chapter, this method also applies to the study of viruses, fungi, and protozoa.

Chapter Overview:

A. Develop a good understanding of the general properties of organisms.

B. Differentiate characteristics between groups of organisms.

C. Consolidate information into charts to highlight comparisons.

D. Differentiate characteristics between specific organisms from different groups.

E. Think clinically by reviewing clinical cases.

F. Use mnemonics to aid recall.

G. Review, review, review.

H. Become familiar with the types of examination questions you will be asked.

A. Develop a good understanding of the general properties of organisms.

Learn general properties before studying details about specific organisms. Learning the characteristics common to all members of a particular group of organisms will allow you to apply that information to each of its members. Learning these rules will reduce the amount of information you need to memorize separately for each. Starting at the most general level, learning that all bacteria are prokaryotes, will enable you to attribute features of a prokaryote (no compartmentalized organelles; nucleoid instead of nucleus; cell envelope) to all bacteria. Learning the characteristics common to all cocci (nonflagellated, nonmotile, nonspore-forming) will enable you to make generalizations about staphylococci. Learning that all staphylococci are catalase positive eliminates the need to memorize this fact for each species of staphylococcus you will learn.

B. Differentiate characteristics between groups of organisms.

Study by comparing major relevant features between groups of organisms. A basic chart for staphylococci and streptococci is partially illustrated in **Figure 13.1**.

STAPHYLOCOCCI	STREPTOCOCCI
Gram-positive	Gram-positive
Grape-like clusters of cells	Chains of cells
Catalase +	Catalase -

Figure 13.1

Distinguishing these general characteristics can help you predict correct answers on examination questions, even when all the details of each organism may not be recalled. See if you can predict the answer to the test question below given just the information in **Figure 13.1**.

Upon laboratory examination, an organism was found to be Gram-positive and catalase negative. This organism is:

(A) *Streptococcus pyogenes*

(B) *Staphylococcus epidermidis*

(C) *Staphylococcus saprophyticus*

(D) *Staphylococcus aureus*

Since you know that all staphylococci are catalase positive you can eliminate options B, C, and D without further consideration. The answer to this question is **A**.

C. Consolidate information into charts to highlight comparisons.

Create charts actively to help you learn. Pay attention to similarities and differences among *groups* of organisms first and then differentiate between specific organisms within groups. A chart created for learning *Staphylococcus species* is illustrated in **Figure 13.2**.

Staphylococci			
Organism	Laboratory Findings	Diseases	Therapeutic Agents
S. aureus	• coagulase + • β-hemolytic	• Food poisoning • Toxic shock syndrome • Localized skin abscesses • Osteomyelitis • Wound infections • Mastitis • Endocarditis • Pneumonia	• Usually penicillin resist. • Vancomycin if altered PBP gives methicillin resist.
S. epidermidis	• coagulase - • no hemolysis	• Nosocomial: catheters • Endocarditis	• Resistant • Use novobiocin
S. saprophyticus	• coagulase - • no hemolysis	• Urinary tract infections	• Penicillin G

Figure 13.2

The best method for memorizing this information is:

- First learn and study one organism to provide an anchor (*Staphylococcus aureus*).

- Then compare a similar organism, *S. epidermidis*, to the anchor. Ask yourself: "How does it differ from *S. aureus*?"

- Next learn *S. saprophyticus*. Ask yourself: "How does it differ from *S. aureus* and from *S. epidermidis*?"

D. Differentiate characteristics between specific organisms from different groups.

Organisms from different groups often have some similar features or characteristics. Compare the charts you prepare for each group of organisms to one another. For example, when comparing staphylococci and streptococci, ask: "Which types of staphylococci and streptococci are β-hemolytic?" "Which can be treated with penicillin G?" "Which are bacitracin sensitive?" Making these explicit comparisons during study is a useful way to organize information needed for examinations.

E. Think clinically by reviewing clinical cases.

Some diseases may be caused by more than one organism. Both meningitis and endocarditis are examples of this. Therefore, you need to compare all the organisms that cause a given disease to clarify how each can be identified and differentiated. What signs and symptoms are present in the patient? What laboratory features are present when the organism is examined microscopically? What treatment is suggested? Review clinical cases and questions that require a diagnosis to help you improve your skills in this area.

F. Use mnemonics to aid recall.

Mnemonics can sometimes be useful. As mentioned in Chapter 3, to remember the names of the viruses that cause gastroenteritis, a student created the acronym: NO ROAD GAS, in which each two letter sequence denotes a virus (NO = Norwalk, RO = rota-, and AD = adeno-) and GAS denotes gastroenteritis. Students also create visual images to incorporate key information about each organism. For example, creating an image of Aunt Penny (penicillin G) shooting (fighting) a large heart (rheumatic fever) may help you associate and recall that penicillin G can be used to treat streptococcal infections and prevent rheumatic fever. When creating such images it is useful to:

- Make all the elements of the picture fit the same theme.

- Use the same representation for a particular property in all of your pictures. For example, if you decide to use Aunt Penny to represent an organism that is killed by penicillin, then use Aunt Penny in all the pictures of organisms that are killed by penicillin.

- Make sure that you can account for every detail on your picture and that nothing extraneous is included.

- Use humor whenever possible to increase memorability.

G.   Review, review, review.

The study materials you create must be reviewed regularly. Set goals for review (e.g., review staphylococci and streptococci) to insure that you reinforce your knowledge of the information sufficiently. Cumulative review, described in Chapter 3, is most effective. For example, when learning to differentiate staphylococci and streptococci, study as follows:

Study Block 1	Compare and contrast the general characteristics of staph. and strep.
Study Block 2	1. Review comparisons of staph. and strep. 2. Compare and contrast characteristics of different types of staph.
Study Block 3	1. Review comparisons of staph. and strep. 2. Review comparisons of different types of staph. 3. Compare and contrast characteristics of different types of strep.

You would continue a similar schedule until you felt confident about your ability to differentiate these organisms.

H. Become familiar with the types of examination questions you will be asked.

- **Microbiology questions require that you are able to use laboratory and clinical information to identify organisms and determine the most likely cause of a patient's symptoms.**

A mother brings her 10-year-old son for a sick visit. He has a fever of 102° F. and is complaining of difficulty breathing. His cough produces thick green sputum. He was diagnosed with cystic fibrosis at 6. Over the past two years, you have treated him five times for similar episodes. A Gram stain of the sputum reveals Gram-negative rods. Which of the following organisms is the most likely cause of his infection?

(A) *Neisseria meningitidis* (meningococcus)

(B) *Staphylococcus aureus*

(C) *Streptococcus pneumoniae*

(D) *Haemophilus influenzae*

(E) *Pseudomonas aeruginosa*

Discussion: *Pseudomonas aeruginosa* are Gram-negative rods that cause a variety of infections including those in the lungs, urinary tract, and wounds in patients with lowered host defenses and cystic fibrosis. Answer: **E**.

- **Microbiology questions require that you understand principles of basic bacteriology.**

Which of the following statements about cell walls of Gram-positive and Gram-negative bacteria is true?

(A) Gram-positive bacteria have a much thicker peptidoglycan layer than Gram-negative bacteria.

(B) All Gram-negative bacteria express teichoic acids.

(C) Gram-positive bacteria release endotoxin, a lipopolysaccharide.

(D) Gram-negative bacteria lack a periplasmic space and outer membrane.

(E) Neither Gram-positive nor Gram-negative bacteria have an outer capsule.

Discussion:

The cell wall is the outermost component in both Gram-negative and Gram-positive bacteria; however, the structure, chemical composition, and thickness of their cell walls differ. Gram-positive bacteria have a much thicker peptidolgycan layer, allowing them to retain more of the Gram stain. They may also express teichoic acids. Only Gram-negative bacteria have a periplasmic space (where b-lactamases are found) and an endotoxin-containing outer membrane. Answer: **A.**

- **Microbiology questions require that you know the basics of vaccine usage and antimicrobial therapy.**

Which of the following is a toxoid vaccine?

  (A) *Neisseria meningitidis* vaccine

  (B) *Haemophilus influenzae* vaccine

  (C) *Clostridium tetani* vaccine

  (D) *Streptococcus pneumoniae* vaccine

  (E)   *Bordetella pertussis* vaccine

Discussion:

A toxoid vaccine contains an inactivated protein exotoxin (toxoid) that provides protection against the naturally occurring toxin. The *Clostridium tetani* vaccine is part of the usual childhood vaccination (part of the DPT or DaPT combination) with regular boosters throughout life. It is also given following a possible exposure to toxin if immunity has lapsed or the vaccine schedule is unknown. Answer: **C.**

- **Microbiology questions require that you understand the life cycle, replication, and routes of infection of various organisms.**

Which of the following organisms is transmitted via the fecal-oral route?

  (A) *Vibrio cholerae*

  (B) *Clostridium tetani*

  (C) *Haemophilus influenzae*

  (D) *Treponema pallidum*

  (E) *Neissaria meningitidis*

Discussion:

Vibrio cholerae is a Gram-negative rod that causes cholera, a severe, watery diarrhea. Cholera can lead to dehydration, electrolyte imbalance, and cardiac and renal failure. It is a major source of morbidity and mortality worldwide. Cholera is transmitted by fecal contamination of water and food or by ingestion of contaminated shellfish. Answer: **A**.

CHAPTER 14

STRATEGIES FOR STUDYING NEUROSCIENCE AND NEUROANATOMY

Neuroscience is the detailed study of the central and peripheral nervous systems. This includes learning the function of neurons and other brain cells, the pathways of "special senses" (vision, hearing, taste, smell, and touch), and mental processes, such as speech, planning, and memory. You will learn about the function of brain cells and the pathways of nerves from "beginning" to "end." You will also need to understand the normal functions of neurons and their systems, and how lesions disrupt functioning.

Neuroanatomy, an important component of neuroscience, is the study of the structures of the brain, brain stem, and cranial nerves. Like Gross Anatomy, it is a visual subject and requires that you memorize vocabulary, visualize structures relative to other structures, and understand the connections between structures.

Chapter Overview

A. Since Neuroanatomy is a visual subject, use words to guide you through the pictures.

B. Learn terminology in a meaningful way. The words will often direct you.

C. Pay attention to the relative locations of structures, how each structure fits in with surrounding structures.

D. Use illustrations and diagrams to consolidate and organize information and to aid in developing conceptualization of the material

E. Identify an anchor point and build your knowledge around it. Learn major pathways in a simplified form.

F. Draw major pathways from memory to see how well you know them.

G. Review cumulatively.

H. Use Neuroanatomy laboratory time efficiently.

I. Become familiar with the types of examination questions you will be asked.

A.   Since Neuroanatomy is a visual subject, use words to guide you through the pictures.

As with Gross Anatomy, Neuroanatomy requires that you make connections between written and pictorial information. It is useful to read the paragraphs in a Neuroanatomy textbook while referring to accompanying figures and pictures. A helpful strategy is to annotate the pictures with information from the text. Visual materials are also useful when gaining understanding of why certain injuries cause specific constellations of symptoms.

B.   Learn terminology in a meaningful way. The words will often direct you.

The central nervous system (CNS) is divided into two main organizational and functional divisions: *ascending information* (sensory information from the body to be interpreted in the brain) and *descending commands* (motor commands from the brain to be carried out by the body). Signals travel within the spinal cord along distinct pathways, and are referred to by their location within the spinal cord or from their starting and end points in the brain and spinal cord. By learning a few key landmarks, the names of many of the pathways become predictable. This is illustrated in Figure **14.1**.

NAME OF PATHWAY	COURSE OF PATHWAY
Dorsal column/ Medial lemniscus	Located in the dorsal (posterior) aspect of the spinal cord and crosses at the medial lemniscus.
Corticospinal	Runs from the *cortex* to the *spinal cord*
Spinothalamic	Runs from the *spinal cord* to *thalamus*
Hypothalomospinal	Runs from the *hypothalamus* to the *spinal cord*

Figure 14.1

The names of pathways also reveal insight into the direction that the pathways take and, therefore, to their function, as illustrated in **Figure 14.2**.

C. Pay attention to the relative locations of structures, how each structure fits in with surrounding structures.

Neuroanatomy, a large component of Neuroscience, requires visualizing structures and regions of the brain and nervous system and their placement in relation to one another. This is difficult, as structures are often small and poorly delineated. To complicate matters, structures must be identified in three views: (1) midsagittal (shows relationship of structures surrounding the third and fourth ventricles), (2) coronal (shows superior/inferior relationships), and (3) axial (shows anterior/posterior relationships). It is important to

PATHWAY	DIRECTION	FUNCTION
Dorsal Column/ Medial lemniscus pathway	From spine to brain (ascending pathway)	Carries sensory information from the body to the cortex for: Light touch Vibration Limb-position sense
Corticospinal tract	From brain to spine (descending pathway)	Mediates voluntary motor activity for skeletal muscles
Spinothalamic tract	From spine to brain (ascending pathway)	Carries sensory information from the body for: Pain Temperature
Hypothalomo-spinal tract	From brain to spine (descending pathway)	Integrates vision with the autonomic nervous system

Figure 14.2

identify structures in each of these views and to develop a 3D understanding of each structure in relation to other regional structures. This can be achieved through "hands-on" manipulation in the Neuroanatomy lab, by using plastic models, or by referencing multiple images in an atlas. **Figures 14.3** and **14.4** illustrate different views (in this case, coronal and axial) of the structures in the brain.

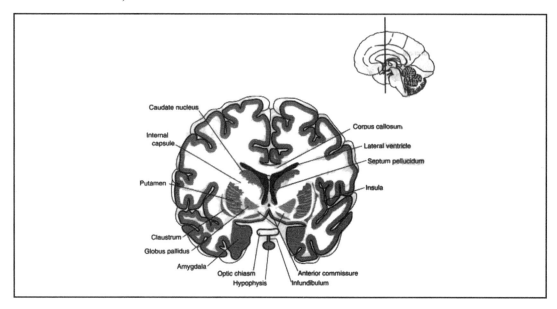

Figure 14.3 Coronal View of the Brain
From: Fix, J.D. (1995). *High-Yield Neuroanatomy*. Williams & Wilkins, p. 2.

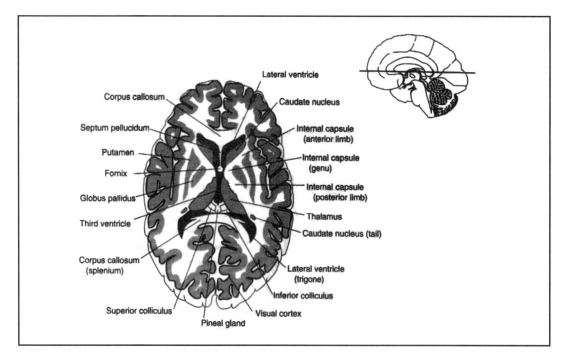

Figure 14.4 Axial View of the Brain
From: Fix, J.D. (1995). *High-Yield Neuroanatomy*. Williams & Wilkins, p. 3.

D. Use illustrations, charts, and diagrams to consolidate and organize information and to aid in developing conceptualization of the material.

Illustrations, charts, and diagrams capture essential relationships and aid in making the information more meaningful because they serve as concise summaries of information. For example, an illustration is very useful when trying to understand how specific lesions will result in clinical pathology. In **Figure 14.5** lesions to the visual system and their associated defects are illustrated. For example, a lesion to the optic nerve (point 1 on the diagram on the left) leads to complete blindness in the eye on the affected side, as shown in the first row of the diagram on the right. (The area of the usual deficit is depicted in black.) A lesion to the optic chiasm (point 2) leads to the visual deficit as shown in row 2, etc. Rather then trying to memorize a list of associated symptoms, better understanding can be gained by incorporating visual information.

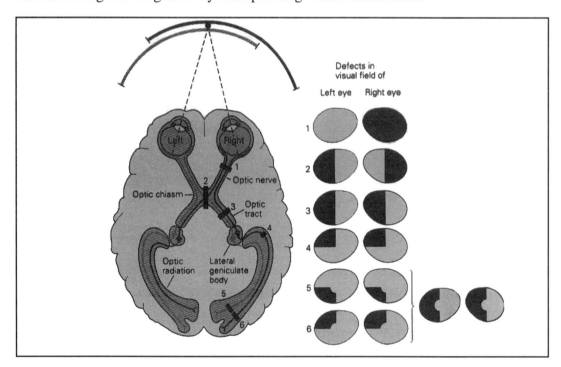

Figure 14.5 Lesions in the Visual System and Associated Defects
From: Kandel, R., Schwartz, J.H. & Jessell, T.M. (2000). *Principles of Neural Science*, p. 544.

Figure 14.6 depicts the hemisection of the spinal cord (also known as Brown-Séquard syndrome.) This leads to the characteristic findings of spastic muscle paralysis and the loss of touch, vibration and position sense on the same side (ipsilateral). You will also see the loss of pain (analgesia) and temperature sense on the opposite side (contralateral) of the lesion.

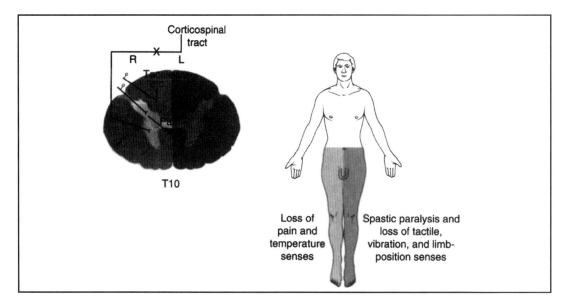

Figure 14.6 Left-Sided Hemisection of the Spinal Cord at T-10
From: Young, P.A. & Young, P. H. (1997). *Basic Clinical Neuroanatomy*, Williams & Wilkins, p. 261.

E. Identify an anchor point and build your knowledge around it. Learn major pathways in a simplified form first.

In Neuroscience you will learn about the normal functioning of individual neurons and the functioning of complex neuronal systems, such as cortical function (planning, language, abstraction), special sensation (sight, taste, hearing), coordination, learning, and memory. Using this knowledge of *normal processes* as an anchor point will enhance understanding of how lesions to the peripheral and central nervous systems disrupt normal function. Some of these lesions will be described in textbooks and lectures. For others, you will need to reason in order to predict defects.

The pathway involved with sight begins in the eye and terminates in the visual cortex, located in the occipital lobe. Learning and recalling the details of this pathway will be easier if you consider it in a simplified form first (your anchor points), and then add "layers" of details later. First learn major locations along the route and then add more specific details. There is an increasing amount of integration and organization of the raw sensory input as a message travels away from the eye toward the visual cortex. For example, the retinal cells (rods and cones) that are initially stimulated in response to single photons of light are grouped into increasing levels of organization that allow us to see the world first in shadows, then in lines, motion, shapes, and colors. These "signals" are then organized according to the area in the field of vision that they originated in, before terminating in the cortex for higher level processing.

F.   Draw major pathways from memory to see how well you know them.

As with Gross Anatomy, this can be a useful step in memorization. For example, when you view the corticospinal tract in an atlas, you may think you can recognize the details. However, to see if you really know the corticospinal tract, try to draw it from memory. If you can draw it, you will be able to identify it and make inferences from your knowledge.

G.   Review cumulatively.

It will be essential to review cumulatively as you proceed through the Neuroscience course. Your success in learning complex concepts will depend on building a solid understanding of the earlier topics.

H.   Use Neuroanatomy laboratory time efficiently.

Effective time spent in the Neuroanatomy laboratory can enhance learning. Some suggestions to help you get the most out of the laboratory time are:

- Use your atlas, models, and textbook to preview so that you know what to expect.

- Set realistic goals for yourself and your group. Will you be able to find and remember all of the structures examined in the laboratory session? Or is it better to learn fewer structures at first and then learn more later?

- Learn actively. Don't stand back and let others do all of the dissecting or identification.

- Locate structures on more than one brain and in more than one section. Structures can vary in size, location, and clarity from one brain to the next.

- Review and clarify. End each laboratory session with a review of the structures just dissected and identified. Begin the next session with a review of structures dissected and identified in the previous session.

- When reviewing, pay attention to the function of a structure, in addition to its location.

- Set up a "practice practical" with a group of students. Include a variety of specimens and different sections (midsagittal, coronal and axial.) Remember, your real practical examination is likely to have only a few questions, if any, tagged on your own specimen.

I.   Become familiar with the types of examination questions you will be asked.

- **Neuroanatomy questions require that you know the location and function of a brain structure or pathway.**

Receptive aphasia is caused by a lesion of:

    (A)   The posterior part of superior temoral gyrus (the Wernicke area)

    (B)   The inferior part of the calcarine sulcus (the Meyer loop)

    (C)   The posterior part of the inferior frontal gyrus (the Broca area)

    (D)   The primary auditory cortex

    (E)   The cochlear nerve (Cranial Nerve VIII)

Discussion:

Damage to the Wernicke area in the dominant hemisphere results in a receptive aphasia with impaired comprehension. (The patient cannot understand any form of language and has speech that is fluent and rapid, but does not make sense). Damage to the Broca area results in an expressive aphasia with intact comprehension. The patient understands both written and spoken language but can not articulate speech or write normally. Damage to the cochlear nerve results in nerve deafness, a deficiency in the perception of sound. Answer: **A**.

- **Neuroscience questions require knowledge of the functional anatomy of the brain stem and spinal cord.**

Which of the following statements about the brain stem and spinal cord is true?

(A) The lateral spinothalamic pathway mediates tactile discrimination, vibration sensation, form recognition, and conscious proprioception.

(B) The dorsal column-medial lemniscus pathway gives rise to axons that cross in the ventral white commissure and ascend in the contralateral lateral funiculus.

(C) In the brainstem, the spinothalamic tract is supplied by the anterior spinal, basilar, and posterior cerebral arteries.

(D) The lateral corticospinal tract terminates on the contra-lateral cerebral cortex.

(E) The intermediolateral cell column, which mediates the entire sympathetic innervation of the body, runs from C1 to L3.

Discussion:

The lateral corticospinal tract, which mediates voluntary motor activity, crosses the midline at the pyramidal decussation and terminates in the contra-lateral motor cortex (precentral gyrus). A small amount of motor activity is mediated by the ventral corticospinal tract which crosses in the ventral white commissure at the level of innervation and also terminates in the contra-lateral motor cortex. Answer: **D**.

- **Neuroscience questions require that you understand the etiology and clinical features of important brain, cranial nerve, and spinal cord lesions.**

A 37-year-old man is hit by a car while crossing the street and is brought to the emergency room. Your exam finds the following:

- Ipsilateral loss of tactile discrimination, position sensation, and vibration sensation below the lesion.

- Ipsilateral spastic paresis with pyramidal signs below the lesion and ipsilateral flaccid paralysis at the level of the lesion.

- Contralateral loss of pain and temperature sensation one segment below the lesion.

Considered together, the symptoms are best explained by which of these lesions?

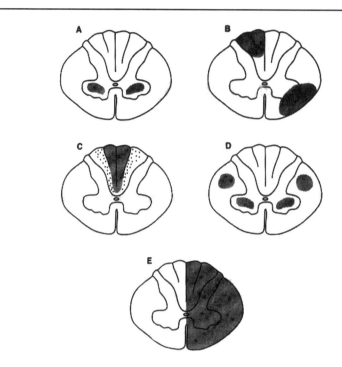

Discussion:

Figure 14.6 in the chapter illustrates the hemisection of the spinal cord (Brown-Séquard syndrome). This results in the symptoms described due to disruption of the dorsal columns, lateral corticospinal tract, lateral spinothalamic tract, ventral horn. If the level of the lesion is above T1, ipsilateral Horner's syndrome may also result due to the disruption of the hypothalamospinal tract. Answer: **E.**

Illustrations from: Fix, J.D. (1995). *High-Yield Neuroanatomy.* Williams & Wilkins, p. 36.

• **Neuroanatomy questions require that you understand the sequence and significance of embryonic events.**

Incomplete closure of the anterior neuropore, and thus failure of the lamina terminalis to develop, results in:

   (A)   Spina bifida

   (B)   Anencephaly

   (C)   Dandy-Walker syndrome

   (D)   Hydrocephalus

   (E)   Arnold-Chiari syndrome

Discussion:

The incomplete closure of the anterior neuropore leads to anencephaly, a failure of the brain to develop. (The incomplete closure of the posterior neuropore leads to spina bifida, a defect of the vertebral arches, meninges, and/or spinal cord usually found in the lumbar/sacral area.) Answer: **B**.

- **Neuroanatomy questions require that you understand the blood supply of the brain and neurologic deficits corresponding to various vascular occlusions.**

A 74-year-old female comes to your office with a complaint of dizziness that began early in the morning. The patient states that her dizziness continued throughout the day, she dropped several items, and noticed bumping into things. She is currently complaining of hoarseness and difficulty swallowing, in addition to the dizziness and clumsiness. Your exam reveals a loss of pain and temperature sensations on the left side of her body and right side of her face and a constricted right pupil. These symptoms are most likely the result of occlusion to which of the following?

(A)   Right posterior cerebral artery

(B)   Basilar artery

(C)   Right posterior inferior cerebellar artery

(D)   Left vertebral artery

(E)   Right internal carotid artery

Discussion:

The posterior inferior cerebellar artery arises from the vertebral branch of the subclavian artery and supplies the dorsolateral quadrant of the medulla, including the nucleus ambiguus (Cranial Nerve IX, X, and XI) and the inferior surface of the cerebellum. Loss of blood supply to these regions best accounts for the patient's symptoms. Answer: **C**.

- **Neuroscience questions may require that you interpret brain MRI/CT scans, including identifying morphologic changes in disease states.**

A 57-year-old woman comes to your office complaining of transient problems with her vision. On exam, you find rapid eye movements (nystagmus), a slight intention tremor, and loss in her visual field. You send her for a MRI of the brain. The finding of *multiple, asymmetric, periventricular lesions* that enhance with gadolinium on MRI is most consistent with the diagnosis of:

(A)   Guillain-Barré syndrome

(B)   Alzheimer disease

(C)   Amyotrophic lateral sclerosis

(D)   Multiple sclerosis

(E)   Poliomyelitis

Discussion:

Multiple sclerosis (MS) is an acquired demyelinating disease of the CNS that presents with varied symptoms (limb weakness, visual disturbances, urinary retention, and dizziness etc.) The MRI findings described are commonly seen in patients with MS. Answer: **D.**

CHAPTER 15

STRATEGIES FOR STUDYING PATHOLOGY

Pathology is the study of the structural and functional changes in cells, tissues, and organs that are seen in various disease states. Pathology utilizes basic science information (learned in your Microbiology, Physiology, Gross and Microscopic Anatomy courses) to help explain the clinical manifestations (signs and symptoms) of disease. Therefore, it requires being able to apply a wide variety of specific principles and mechanisms learned in other courses to a variety of disease states in many different organ systems. A key to success is to solidify your knowledge of the essentials (e.g., general information about the most common disease processes) before beginning more detailed study.

Chapter Overview

A. Develop a framework for the material

B. Identify the most important/common disease processes within each subject area.

C. Learn the most important/common things first.

D. Look for relationships. Don't just learn facts.

E. Learn key characteristics and/or pathognomic features that suggest diagnoses.

F. Become familiar with the types of examination questions you will be asked.

A.   Develop a framework for the material.

Look at the whole chapter of your textbook to see how it is organized before you begin reading. Getting the big picture will help you classify material. For example, **Figure 15.1** highlights major categories of lung diseases.

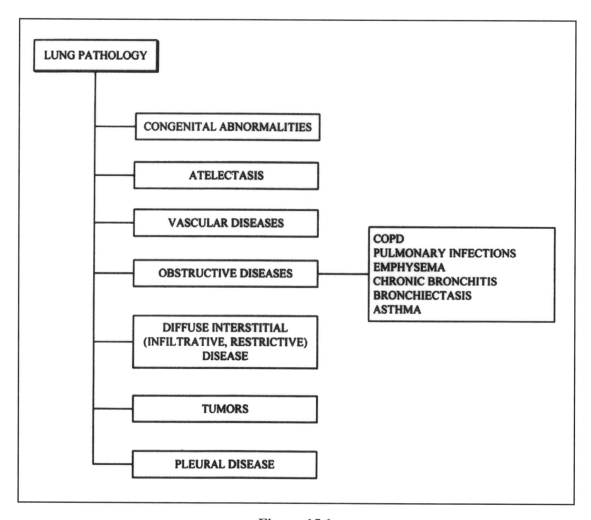

Figure 15.1

When diseases pertain to anatomic regions, organizing information according to region is useful. **Figure 15.2**, a picture of the female genital tract, illustrates that writing the disease categories onto a picture of the organs is an effective way to organize this type of information.

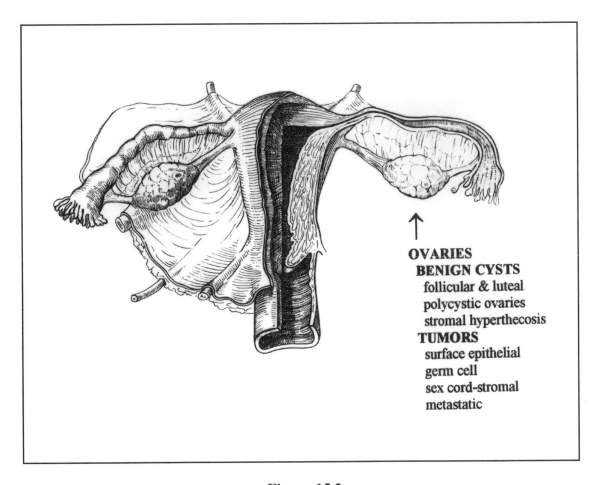

OVARIES
  BENIGN CYSTS
    follicular & luteal
    polycystic ovaries
    stromal hyperthecosis
  TUMORS
    surface epithelial
    germ cell
    sex cord-stromal
    metastatic

Figure 15.2

B.   Identify the most important/common disease processes in each subject area.

All organ systems have essentially the same general types of diseases—congenital abnormalities, tumors, parenchymal diseases, and the like. But in each organ system some diseases are considered more important than others. For instance, when studying diseases of the bowel, inflammatory conditions (like ulcerative colitis and Crohn disease) are likely to get much more coverage than congenital abnormalities. These are more common diseases and have characteristics that make them fairly representative examples of gastrointestinal diseases. For each system, try to organize material according to what the most important topics are likely to be. Then divide up the time you give each subject/disease using your priority list to guide you.

C.   Learn the most important/common diseases first.

This idea is a natural outgrowth of B above. Learn the most common or most important diseases first. Remember the frame approach (Chapter 1). Even though you may feel there is no way to learn all the material in the time allotted, by focusing on the general information first and successively adding levels of detail, you can get the most out of your studying. For example, **Figure 15.3** is a representation of the frame method applied to the study of diseases of the cardiovascular system.

Pass One: learn the types of diseases	Pass Two: learn the major disease in each category	Pass Three: identify the most common or most important diseases in each group for detailed study
Ischemic	• angina • myocardial infarction	• both
Endocarditic	• bacterial endo. • viral endo. • marantic endo. • carcinoid endo.	• bacterial endo.
Valvular	• prolapse • stenosis • insufficiency	• mitral prolapse • aortic stenosis
Congenital	• rubella • ASD • VSD • tetralogy of Fallot	• VSD
Cardiomyopathic	• dilated • restrictive • hypertrophic	• dilated

Figure 15.3

It is essential to assess regularly what the most important/most common disease is and what features characterize this disease.

D. Look for relationships. Don't just learn a collection of facts.

You will recall the material more easily if you draw comparisons between different disease processes. For example, when studying glomerular renal diseases, an important set of general distinctions can be made between the nephrotic and the nephritic syndromes as shown in **Figure 15.4**.

NEPHROTIC SYNDROME	NEPHRITIC SYNDROME
• Heavy proteinuria (> 3.5g/d) • Hypoalbuminemia • Edema • Hyperlipidemia	• Hematuria • Oliguria • Azotemia • Hypertension

Figure 15.4

Learning these distinctions will help you remember the differences between individual diseases (e.g., membranous glomerulonephritis and focal segmental glomerulosclerosis.) Similarly, when studying specific diseases (like Crohn disease and ulcerative colitis) learn both the similarities (both cause diarrhea) as well as the differences (in ulcerative colitis only the mucosa is affected).

E. Learn key characteristics and/or pathognomonic features that can suggest diagnoses.

You will sometimes find that the only memorable difference between one disease and another is a pathognomonic histological finding or a key feature that is used only in connection with a certain disease. Knowing this can help you learn to distinguish two similar diseases. **Figure 15.5** lists some diseases and their associated key characteristics or pathognomonic features.

Key Characteristics of Various Diseases

Disease	Key Characteristic/ Pathognomonic Feature
· membranoproliferative glomerulonephritis	· "tram-track" appearance
· poststreptococcal glomerulonephritis	· "lumpy bumpy" appearance
· amyloidosis	· Congo red/green birefringence
· alcoholic hepatitis	· Mallory bodies
· Crohn disease	· skin lesions
· chronic myelogenous leukemia	· Philadelphia chromosome

Figure 15.5

F. Become familiar with the types of examination questions you will be asked.

- **Pathology questions require that you identify diseases based on their histologic, etiologic, laboratory, and clinical features.**

A patient comes to your office complaining of brown urine that looks "smoky." She notes that she is producing less urine than usual. She had a sore throat two weeks ago. Blood work shows mild elevation of serum urea nitrogen and creatinine. Her urine reveals red blood cells and red blood cell casts. Microscopic examination of sections of a renal biposy shows a "lumpy bumpy" appearance in the glomerular basement membrane under immunofluorescence. Which of the following is the most likely diagnosis?

(A) Membranous glomerulonephritis

(B) Minimal change disease

(C) Poststreptococcal glomerulonephritis

(D) Focal and segmental glomerulonephritis

(E) Renal amyloidosis

Discussion:

Of the answer choices, only poststreptococcal glomerulonephritis accounts for all of the signs, symptoms, and laboratory findings. It usually follows infection by b-hemolytic streptococci and manifests as the nephrotic syndrome—oligouria (decreased urine output), azotemia (increased serum urea nitrogen and creatinine), hypertension, and hematuria (smoky brown urine. Answer: **C**.

- **Pathology questions require that you understand the role of risk factors in the etiology of disease.**

Which of the following statements regarding risk factors for malignant mesothelioma and bronchogenic carcinoma is true?

- (A) Cigarette smoking does not significantly increase the risk of either disease.

- (B) Malignant mesothelioma is only slightly more common in people with asbestos exposure than in people without asbestos exposure.

- (C) Cessation of smoking for 30 years is not associated with a reduction in the risk of developing bronchogenic carcinoma.

- (D) The risk of asbestos-related mesothelioma is markedly increased in cigarette smokers.

- (E) The risk of asbestos related bronchogenic carcinoma is markedly increased in cigarette smokers.

Discussion:

Bronchogenic carcinoma, the most common form of lung cancer, is the most frequent fatal malignancy in both men and women. It is associated with both smoking and exposure to asbestos. Malignant mesothelioma is less common but is frequently fatal. While mesothelioma is strongly associated with exposure to asbestos, there seems to be no increased risk in smokers. Answer: **E**.

- **Pathology questions require that you understand the etiology of common clinical findings and presentations.**

Cystic fibrosis is a widespread disorder that affects many organ systems. Which of the following best explains why patients with cystic fibrosis are often malnourished?

(A)   Increased loss of essential vitamins and minerals in sweat

(B)   Decreased appetite

(C)   Blockage of biliary apparatus by mucus

(D)   Plugging of pancreatic exocrine glands

(E)   Thickening of the muscular layer of the terminal ileum

Discussion:

The mutation that causes cystic fibrosis leads to a defect in fluid secretion that affects the respiratory, gastrointestinal, and reproductive tracts. Involvement of the pancreatic exocrine glands and ducts can lead to decreased enzyme secretion and resultant steatorrhea, malabsorption, and nutritional deficiencies. Answer: **D.**

- **Pathology questions require that you known the "most common" type, location, or complication of a disease.**

The most common cause of a palpable breast mass in women between the ages of 20 and 50 is:

(A)   Fibroadenoma

(B)   Fibrocystic disease

(C)   Intraductal papilloma

(D)   Inflammatory carcinoma

(E)   Medullary carcinoma

Discussion:

Fibrocystic disease, also referred to as fibrocystic change, is characterized by "lumpy breasts" and midcycle tenderness due to bilateral fibrosis and cystic changes. It is uncommon before adolescence or after menopause. Answer: **B.**

CHAPTER 16

STRATEGIES FOR STUDYING PHARMACOLOGY

Pharmacology is the study of drugs and their interactions with the body. You will learn about the mechanism of action, metabolism, side effects, toxicity, and drug-drug interactions of clinically prescribed medications, herbal remedies, and illicitly used drugs. Because pharmaceutically active substances have such a wide range of uses and effects, mastering Pharmacology requires being able to integrate material from a variety of other courses, such as Pathology, Pathophysiology, and Microbiology. Students often find Pharmacology difficult because it requires the understanding, organization, and application of a large amount of information. Therefore, a key to success is to review relevant basic sciences and clinical topics before beginning to study a new class of drugs.

Chapter Overview

A. Develop a road map for each drug class.

B. Use your knowledge of physiology to understand how specific drugs affect the body.

C. Learn the mechanism of action of the prototypic drug.

D. Use the endings of drug names to help you learn which drugs are in each class.

E. Learn the other drugs in the same class and note how they are different from the prototypic drug.

F. Use cumulative review to enhance memorization.

G. Become familiar with the types of examination questions you will be asked.

A. Develop a road map for each class of drug.

Begin by making an organizational chart of the material you are about to learn. For example, the adrenomimetic agonists are divided into two general categories—direct-acting and indirect-acting. These two categories are further divided into several specific subcategories. Knowing about the categories and subcategories will make it easier to learn where each separate drug fits. **Figure 16.1** shows drugs in the direct-acting group broken down by which receptor they activate (α agonists, β agonists). In the indirect-acting group, the drugs are divided into those that facilitate the release of endogenous adrenergic agents and those that inhibit the reuptake of the endogenous adrenergic agents.

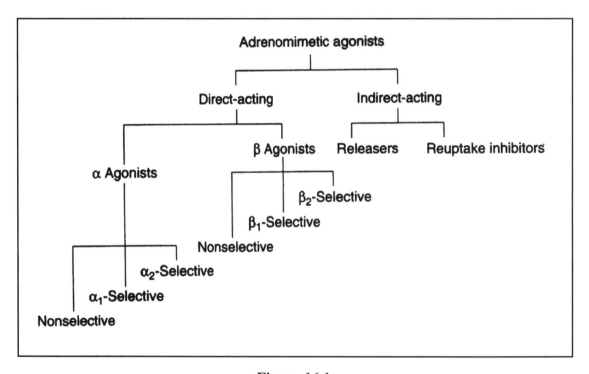

Figure 16.1

From: Katzung, Bertram G. & Trevor, Anthony J. (1995). *Examination & Board Review - Pharmacology*, 4th edition, p. 68. Reprinted by permission of Appleton & Lange.

Road maps for classes of drugs can also be developed based on their therapeutic uses or the organ systems they affect. For example, **Figure 16.2** is a road map that organizes the diuretics by their sites of action in the kidney.

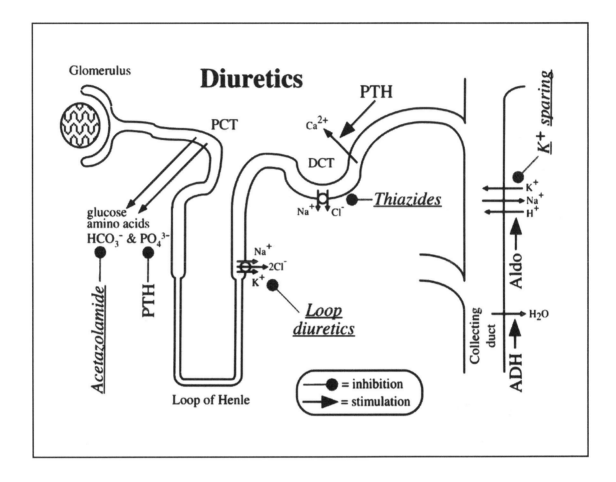

Figure 16.2

From: Johannsen, Eric C. & Sabatine, Marc S. *PharmCards*, Card #4: "Diuretics." Reprinted by permission of Lippincott-Raven.

B. Use your knowledge of physiology to understand how specific drugs affect the body.

It is best to learn the consequences of activation of a particular organ system or receptor type before getting into the details of the drugs. For example, when learning the adrenergic agonists, organizing the prototypic information as illustrated in **Figure 16.3** will be helpful.

Adrenergic Stimulation	
Organ/System	Effect
Eye	• α_1: contracts pupillary dilator muscle $\rightarrow$ mydriasis
Vascular Smooth Muscle	• α_1: contractions $\rightarrow$ $\uparrow$ peripheral resistance
Adrenergic & Cholinergic Nerve Terminals	• α_2: $\downarrow$ transmitter release
Fat Cells	• α_2: $\downarrow$ lipolysis
Heart	• β_1: $\uparrow$ rate & force
Renal	• pancreatic β cells & juxtaglomerular cells: β_1: $\uparrow$ renin release • renal blood vessels: D_1: relaxation $\rightarrow$ vasodilation
Respiratory, Vascular & Uterine Smooth Muscle	• β_2: relaxation $\rightarrow$ bronchodilation, uterine and vascular smooth muscle relaxation

Figure 16.3

By learning the effects of specific receptor stimulation, you will gain a physiologic understanding of the class of drugs. These prototypic actions usually coincide with a certain bioactive substance or substances—in this case, epinephrine, norepinephrine, and dopamine. Learning the drugs is a matter of categorizing them based on the effect they have on the system (e.g., they turn it on or off), on what part of the system they affect (e.g., they activate peripheral receptors but not central receptors), and so forth.

C.   Learn the mechanism of action of the prototypic drug.

Each class of drug has a prototype. It might be the first drug developed for a specific clinical purpose, the drug within a category with the widest range of action, or the most effective drug in a category. Learn the prototypic drug in detail to gain a solid foundation on the effects of a particular class of drug. Categories you will find useful for learning drugs are listed below in **Figure 16.4**.

Category	Meaning	Comments
Mechanism	This is how the drug works, where the drug acts, and the basic consequences of that action.	This will be a long list for some drugs (like the adrenergics) and a short list for others (like the anesthetics).
Clinical Uses	This is how the drug is used therapeutically.	Since many drugs can be used across classes of action (i.e., as a sedative-hypnotic & as an antiepileptic), it is useful to define when this drug is the drug of choice for something.
Toxicities & Side Effects	This is a listing of the undesired actions of the drug.	It is important to note that sometimes the undesired actions of a drug for one use are the desired actions of the same drug for another use.
Metabolism	This is the method of admin-istration, how the drug is cleared from the body, etc.	It is very important to note if the drug induces or inhibits the metabolism of other drugs or if it interacts with drugs of other classes.
Resistance	This is a listing of the things that may block a drug from working effectively.	This category is important in the study of cancer chemotherapy, antimicrobials, and other anti-infectious agents.

Figure 16.4

Figure 16.5 is a chart for epinephrine, the prototype for the adrenergic agonists. Once you have learned the actions of epinephrine (the prototype of this class), your work in learning the remainder of the adrenergic agonists will be substantially reduced.

Drug	Mechanism	Clinical Uses	Toxicities, Side Effects, Contraindications
Epinephrine	• hits α_1, α_2, β_1, β_2 • α_1: vascular smooth mm. contraction • α_2: inhibits adrenergic NT release • β_1: ↑HP, ⊕ inotrope • β_2: broncho- & coronary aa. dilation	• anaphylaxis, shock • asthma • nasal decongestant • causes mydriasis	side effects: • HTN • MI CI: • narrow angle glaucoma • shock • labor

Figure 16.5

D.   Use the endings of drug names to help you learn which drugs are in each class.

Most drug names are consistent within a class. Memorizing all the long names is therefore not usually necessary as you can just identify the ending of the name that is specific to a particular class. Of course, the exceptions will have to be learned. (**Figure 16.6**)

Drug Class	Common Ending	Example	Exception
β-blockers	-olol	propranolol	No important ones
Adrenergic Agonists	-phrine	epinephrine	Clonidine
Benzodiazepines	-pam	diazepam	Chlordiazepoxide
Barbiturates	-tal	phenobarbital	No important ones
Nondepolarizing Skeletal Muscle Relaxants	-curium -curonium	atracurium pancuronium	Tubocurarine
Tricyclic Antidepressants	-tyline -pramine	nortriptyline imipramine	Doxepin

Figure 16.6

E.   Learn the other drugs in the same class and how they are different from the prototypic drug.

When you know the actions of the prototype, you can assume the same actions for all the other drugs of the class, with some exceptions. The exceptions must be learned. **Figure 16.7** expands on the information presented in **Figure 16.5**. The information included in the chart differentiates each drug from the prototype, epinephrine.

F.   Use cumulative review to enhance memorization.

Reviewing the charts you create is essential to learning pharmacology. Be certain to review old material before adding new material.

Drug	Mechanism	Clinical Uses	Toxicities, Side Effects, Contraindications
Epinephrine	• hits α_1, α_2, β_1, β_2 • α_1: vascular smooth mm. contraction • α_2: inhibits adrenergic NT release • β_1: ↑HP, ⊕ inotrope • β_2: broncho- & coronary aa. dilation	• anaphylaxis, shock • asthma • nasal decongestant • causes mydriasis	side effects: • HTN • MI CI: • narrow angle glaucoma • shock • labor
Norepinephrine	• hits $\alpha_1 = \alpha_2 \rangle \beta_2$ • ∅ β_2 • ↓ HR b/c of reflex vagal response	• septic chock • other hemodynamic compromise	• anxiety • respiratory distress • arrhythmias • etc.
Dopamine	• $D_1 = D_2 \rangle \beta_1 \rangle \beta_2$ • D_1: renal vasodilation • ∅ very good bronchodilator ($\beta2$)	• CHF • shock • etc.	side effects: • arrhythmias • etc.

Figure 16.7

G.   Become familiar with the types of examination questions you will be asked.

- **Pharmacology questions require that you know the major side effects and toxicity of drugs.**

Which of the following is (are) the most common side effects of phenytoin?

(A)   Dry, hacking cough

(B)   Hepatitis and hepatic failure

(C)   Orthostatic hypotension

(D)   Increase appetite and weight gain

(E)   Nystagmus and ataxia

Discussion:

Phenytoin is used to suppress tonic-clonic and partial seizures. It also has antiarrhythmic properties and can depress cerebellar and vestibular system function. Common side effects include nausea and vomiting, nystagmus, ataxia, megaloblastic anemia, and behavioral changes. In children, gingival hyperplasia and coarsening of facial features may also be seen. Answer: **E.**

- **Pharmacology questions require you to distinguish between similar drugs and that you know their major therapeutic indications.**

A 69-year-old man with a history of congestive heart failure visits you in the office for a routine examination. Although he reports being in his usual state of health, his blood pressure was 200/110. Looking over your notes, you notice that he has had elevated blood pressure during past visits. His current medications include a β-blocker and a daily baby aspirin. The history and physical add no additional information. You decide to add another antihypertensive medication (from a different class) to help control his hypetension. Which of the following antihypertensive drugs is appropriate for this pateint?

- (A) Verapamil
- (B) Nifedipine
- (C) Propranolol
- (D) Timolol
- (E) Hydroxyurea

Discussion:

Nifedipine is a calcium channel blocker that is useful in the treatment of hypertensive patients who are already on a β-blocker or who have asthma, angina, diabetes mellitus, or peripheral vascula disease. Although it is a calcium channel blocker, verapamil should be avoided in patients with a history of congestive heart failure because it has negative inotropic effects, i.e., it limits the strength of cardiac contractions. Answer: **B.**

- **Pharmacology questions require you apply appropriate formulas and perform simple calculations.**

A drug is given with continuous intravenous infusion. The half-life of the drug is 10 hours. How many hours are required for the drug to reach 90% of its steady-state concentration?

(A) 22 hours

(B) 33 hours

(C) 44 hours

(D) 55 hours

(E) 60 hours

Discussion:

This question requires that you understand that 90% of the steady-state drug concentration is achieved at a time that is 3.3 times the half-life. In this problem, $T_{1/2} \times 3.3 = 10 \times 3.3 = 33$ hours. After 33 hours, this drug will reach 90% of its steady state concentration. Answer: **B**.

- **Pharmacology questions require that you understand the mechanism of action and main physiologic effects of drugs.**

Which of the following statements about the adrenergic drug dobutamine is true?

(A) It has α_1, α_2, β_1, and β_2 receptors.

(B) It has activity at dopaminergic and β_1 receptors.

(C) It is used in the treatment of congestive heart failure (CHF).

(D) It is usually taken orally.

(E) It crosses the blood-brain barrier and acts centrally.

Discussion:

Dobutamine is a direct-acting catecholamine (β_1-receptor agonist) that causes tachycardia and increased cardiac contractility. It is administered intravenously to increase cardiac output in severe CHF because it does not elevate oxygen demands of the myocardium. Dobutamine has activity at dopaminergic and β_1 receptors and is used in the treatment of shock and CHF. Answer: **C**.

Notes

CHAPTER 17

STRATEGIES FOR STUDYING PHYSIOLOGY

Physiology is the study of the dynamic processes that regulate normal bodily function and homeostasis. You will learn about many organ systems including the heart and blood vessels, gastrointestinal system, renal system, endocrine system, and respiratory system. Students often find Physiology challenging but interesting because it provides tangible insights into how the body works. A key to success in Physiology is to maintain a good conceptual understanding of the "bigger picture" while studying the large amounts of specific information you will need to remember.

Chapter Overview

A. Understand that Physiology is the study of the control and regulation of body systems and processes.

B. Use illustrations and diagrams to aid in developing conceptualization of the material.

C. Look for rules to make facts more meaningful.

D. Make sense of the concept behind a formula before trying to learn it.

E. Become familiar with the types of examination questions you will be asked.

A. Understand that physiology is the study of the control and regulation of body systems and processes.

When learning about each system, keep in mind the principles of **set point** and **homeostasis**. Ask yourself:

- *What is the normal state of the system?* For example, when learning the cardiovascular system, it is useful to consider the normal function of the heart (simplified here for illustrative purposes). The heart pumps blood. At the most basic level, the effectiveness of that pump depends upon the rate of the pumping (heart rate) and the size of each pump (stroke volume). These two elements together determine the cardiac output.

- *What is required to maintain normal functioning?* For example, in order for the heart to maintain its normal functioning, it must be adequately perfused with oxygen (which it uses to drive its own metabolic needs), it must have adequate room for expansion within the pericardium (the sac around the heart), and it must be able to expand to a great enough volume between contractions so that a sufficient amount of blood can enter its chambers to be propelled to the rest of the body during contraction. Anything that interferes with these will affect functioning.

- *What normal changes can occur in a system?* When a person exercises, for example, oxygen demand of peripheral tissues increases. The heart must adjust its cardiac output to fit the new needs of the body. This is usually done by increasing either the heart rate or the stroke volume (usually the former dominates). This adjustment in cardiac output increases the work done by the heart as well as the strain on the heart. Similarly, when one finishes exercising, the heart rate slows or the stroke volume decreases to match the decreased metabolic needs of the body.

- *What are the consequences of abnormal functioning?* When the heart must increase output, it does so by increasing the amount of work it does. This puts an increased strain on the heart muscle itself. If the heart is required to maintain these compensatory mechanisms chronically (as often happens after a myocardial infarction), the heart will ultimately fail (congestive heart failure). This results in consequences for the systemic tissues, e.g., a decrease in oxygen perfusion, subsequent oxygen starvation leading to tissue death, and fluid accumulation behind the failing ventricle (pulmonary edema).

B. Use illustrations and diagrams to aid in developing conceptualization of the material.

Illustrations concisely capture essential relationships. Annotating such materials will make the information more meaningful to you. **Figure 17.1** below is a graph that integrates the heart sounds with the EKG. The QRS complex on the EKG signifies that ventricular excitation has occurred. This quickly results in ventricular contraction. As ventricular pressure increases and exceeds atrial pressure, the AV valves close resulting in the first heart sound. This signifies the beginning of ventricular systole. At the onset of ventricular relaxation, the ventricular pressures fall, leading to closure of the aortic and pulmonary (semilunar) valves, resulting in the second heart sound. This signifies the beginning of ventricular diastole.

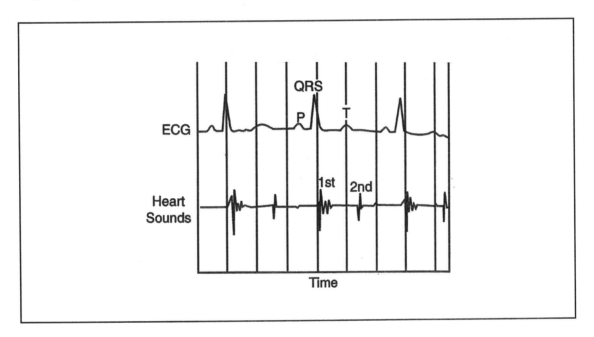

Figure 17.1

From: Berne, R.M. & M.N. Levy (1998) *Physiology*, 4th edition, p. 372. Reprinted by permission of Mosby, Inc.

The graph in **Figure 17.2** illustrates volume-pressure curves in normal and abnormal lungs. Your objective should be to explain what is happening at various points along each of the curves shown. In addition, it is useful to extend your knowledge and consider where the volume-pressure curves for other diseases would lie in relation to these (e.g., asthma, pneumonia, etc.).

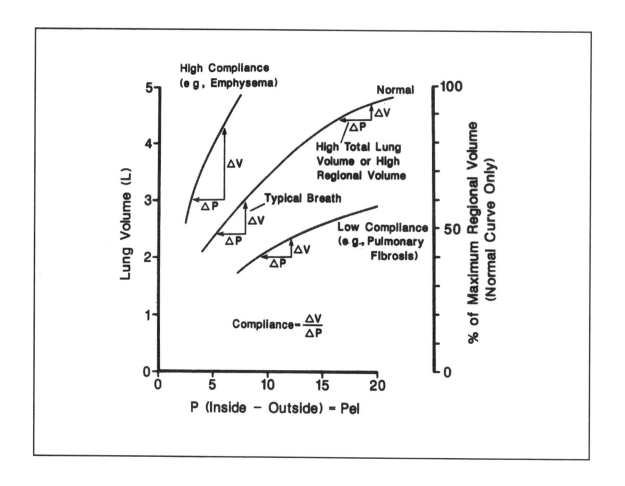

Figure 17.2

From: Thies, R. (1994). *Oklahoma Notes: Physiology*, 3rd edition, p. 121. Reprinted by permission of Springer-Verlag.

C.   Look for rules to make facts more meaningful.

Actively seeking out connections helps to consolidate information and makes material more meaningful. In the cardiac cycle (**Figure 17.1**), valves open and close due to changes in pressure on either side of them. In neurophysiology, depolarization of cell membranes always makes the difference in electric potential between the outside of the cell and the inside of the cell smaller. In endocrinology, hormones that exhibit a permissive effect on the physiology of the body (e.g., thyroid hormone) usually exhibit little effect unless above a certain threshold and exhibit essentially the same effect over their usual physiologic range.

D. Make sense of the concept behind a formula before trying to learn it.

Here is the formula for blood flow:

$$\text{FLOW} = \frac{\Delta \text{ PRESSURE}}{\text{RESISTANCE (R)}} = \frac{\Delta \text{ PRESSURE}}{1/\text{RADIUS}^4}$$

This is one of many formulas you will need to know. Retaining all of these by rote memorization alone is risky, if not impossible. It is more useful to consider intuitively how flow, resistance, pressure, and blood vessel size (radius) relate. A useful analogy to use is one of water running through a pipe of specific radius. (**Figure 17.3**)

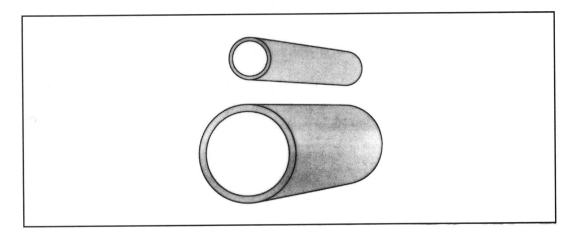

Which has greater resistance?

Figure 17.3

Assuming constant pressure, adding resistance (such as sludge) will hinder the flow. Resistance is also related to vessel size. What will happen to flow if the pipe is replaced by one with a larger radius? How about one with a smaller radius? What would happen if you agitated the water? What would happen if you made the pipe longer? The answer to the following multiple choice question may now be predictable:

Resistance to flow of blood in a vessel will increase if:

(A) the viscosity of the blood is decreased

(B) flow becomes nonturbulent

(C) the vessel length is increased

(D) the vessel diameter is increased

The correct answer is C.

E. Become familiar with the types of examination questions you will be asked.

- **Physiology questions often require that you understand and make predictions about relationships, even if you have not studied them directly.**

Figure 17.4 below represents a pressure-volume loop of the left ventricle for a single cardiac cycle.

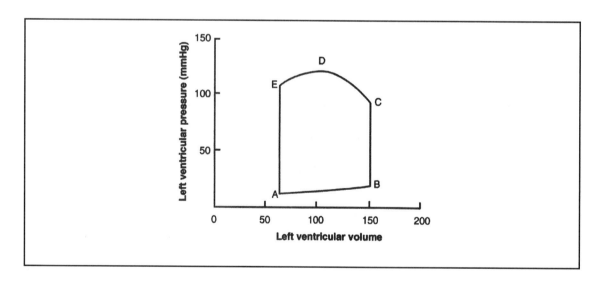

Figure 17.4

From: Barton, T.K. (1993). *Appleton & Lange's Review for the USMLE Step 1*, p. 29. Reprinted by permission of Appleton & Lange.

If aortic pressure is maintained at a constant level, a sudden transfusion of blood will result in a:

(A) shift in B to the left

(B) shift in B to the righ

(C) shift in C to the left

(D) decrease in the area inscribed by ABCDE

(E) decrease in segment CDE

Discussion:

The pressure-volume loop concisely displays the changes in pressure and volume in the left ventricle that occur during a single cycle of systole and diastole. By understanding how the processes of contraction, ejection, relaxation, and refilling are depicted, this figure can be used to make predictions. Therefore, even if you do not directly study the effects of increasing blood volume, e.g., after a transfusion, understanding these principles in the figure allows you to predict that the width of the pressure-volume loop will increase. Answer: **B**.

- **Physiology questions require that you understand clinical findings related to normal and abnormal functioning.**

After sitting several hours while watching a movie, you quickly stand up to leave the theater. Which of the following compensatory changes is most likely to occur to maintain arterial blood pressure?

(A) decreased heart rate

(B) increased cardiac output

(C) increased stroke volume

(D) increase central venous pressure

(E) increased total peripheral resistance

Discussion:

Prolonged sitting causes blood to pool in the veins of the lower extremities because of the effects of gravity and muscular inactivity. This results in a decrease in venous return to the heart (decrease central venous pressure) and therefore, a decrease in cardiac output and in arterial blood pressure. The body compensates for this drop in cardiac output and blood pressure by increasing the heart rate, contractility, and arterial vasoconstriction (total peripheral resistance) through the release of catecholamines. Answer: **E**.

- **Physiology questions require that you apply appropriate formulas and perform simple calculations.**

What is the cardiac output (CO) of a patient whose heart rate (HR) is 72 bpm and whose stroke volume (SV) is 75 mL?

(A)   0.96 L/min

(B)   1.04 L/min

(C)   5.40 L/min

(D)   9.60 L/min

(E)   10.40 L/min

Discussion:

This question requires that you calculate cardiac output using the formula CO = SV X HR. In this problem, CO = 75 mL (SV) X 73 bpm (HR) = 5,400 mL/min = 5.40 L/min. Answer: **C**.

- **Physiology questions require that you understand the function and regulation of organs and major body systems.**

Which of the following is true concerning the hormone gastrin?

(A)   It is secreted by parietal cells in glands of the fundic stomach.

(B)   It is released in response to histamine stimulation.

(C)   It increases the absorption of vitamin B_{12} by the terminal ileum.

(D)   It increases the thickness of the protective gastric mucus.

(E)   It increase the concentration of gastric H^+

Discussion:

This question requires that you understand gastrointestinal physiology. Gastrin is released by G cells located in the gastric antrum in response to food or vagal stimulation. Gastrin is important for gastric function because it increases gastric H^+ (decreases pH). Gastric pepsin has an acidic pH optimum. As the $[H^+]$ increases, it inhibits further gastrin release. This is an example of negative feedback inhibition. Answer: **E**.

PART III

THE USMLE

CHAPTER 18

HOW TO EXCEL
ON THE USMLE

When you successfully complete your basic science courses and your clinical rotations, you will be awarded your degree as a medical doctor, and will be entitled to use the letters M.D. after your name. However, to practice medicine, you must also pass the United States Medical Licensure Examination (USMLE), a three-step examination sponsored by the Federation of State Medical Boards (FSMB) and the National Board of Medical Examiners (NBME). Some medical schools require that you pass the USMLE, Step 1 (a basic science examination) before you proceed through your clinical years, and some require that you pass the USMLE, Step 2 (a clinical science and clinical skills examination) before you are allowed to graduate. The USMLE, Step 3, which completes the examination process for licensure, is usually taken after the first year of residency training is completed. You can find general and specific information about all three steps of the United States Medical Licensure Examination on the web site: http://www.usmle.org.

The strategies detailed in this book will help you successfully complete your basic science courses in medical school and will lead to more durable learning to provide an excellent scientific foundation for your clinical work. Your enhanced ability to "hold on" to what you have learned will also be a big dividend when it is time to prepare for the USMLE, Step 1 examination. However, even if you have retained a great deal, it will be important to prepare in a systematic and organized manner for this important examination, to maximize your performance, and to achieve the highest score possible. This chapter will be your guide.

Chapter Overview

A. The Exam

• What is tested on the USMLE, Step 1?

• What is the structure of the USMLE, Step 1?

• What types of questions are on the exam?

• How is the USMLE, Step 1 scored and reported?

B. Exam Preparation: Factors to Consider

• What study resources shall I use?

• What study strategies are best for review and retention?

• How can I best manage my time?

• What can I do to sustain effort in studying?

• What are the best test-taking strategies?

C. Frequently Asked Questions

• Should I take a review course to prepare for the USMLE, Step 1?

• Should I plan my study by subjects or should I take a "systems" approach?

• When should I begin using questions?

• How many hours a day do I need to spend studying to do well on this exam?

• How should I schedule my study breaks? How much break time should I take?

• Appendix A: Planning Worksheet

• Appendix B: Sample Study Schedules

A. THE EXAM

- **What is tested on the USMLE, Step 1?**

The USMLE, Step 1 is a test of whether you understand and can apply knowledge learned in your basic science courses and includes the following subjects:

- Anatomy (Gross Anatomy, Microscopic Anatomy, Embryology, Neuroanatomy, and Neuroscience)
- Behavioral Science (including Behavioral Science, Psychiatry, Biostatistics, and Epidemiology)
- Biochemistry
- Microbiology (including Cell Biology, Immunology, and Microbiology)
- Pathology
- Pharmacology
- Physiology
- Interdisciplinary topics (Nutrition, Genetics, and Clinical Pathophysiology)

The USMLE, Step 1 includes questions about general principles that are not limited to specific organ systems, and questions concerning normal and abnormal processes that are organ system specific.

- **What is the structure of the USMLE, Step 1?**

The USMLE, Step 1 is a seven-hour, computer-generated, multiple-choice examination. One hour is allotted for breaks. The exam is arranged in 1 hour "blocks" of 50 questions each. On average, the time allotted to answer each question is approximately 80 seconds.

- **What types of questions are on the exam?**

All the questions on the USMLE, Step 1 are formatted as single one best answer multiple-choice type. Many begin with a short clinical scenario followed by 5 or more answer options. The questions are organized in a random mix and many questions have an integrated format, i.e., they will require you to recall information you will have learned in several different courses. You will be asked to interpret pictorial material, including graphs and histologic and pathologic slides. You will be asked to apply the knowledge learned in your basic science courses to clinical problems. However, keep in mind that despite the clinical appearance of the questions, the information you have learned in your basic science courses should be sufficient for determining correct answers.

- **How is the USMLE, Step 1 scored and reported?**

Your score will be based on the number of questions you answer correctly. There are no deductions for incorrect answers. Some questions on this exam will not count toward your score, as new questions are constantly being "tried out." Since there is no way to know which are the trial questions, it is best to approach every question as though it "counts." It is equally important not to spend too much time on the questions that seem a bit odd or confusing. The number of questions you answer correctly will be reported as a two digit and three digit standard score. These two scores are equivalent. The standard passing score has been changed several times since the computerized USMLE, Step 1 was implemented, so you may wish to check the web site periodically to learn what the passing score will be. However, since you will be aiming for the highest score possible, the actual score needed to pass should not influence your preparation strategies. The percent of questions you will need to answer correctly to pass this exam is estimated to be in the 60 to 70% range.

B.   Exam Preparation: Factors to Consider

When studying for the USMLE, Step 1, you will need to review a large amount of information in a limited amount of time. Therefore, your study should be:

√ *Purposeful:* It will be helpful to have a study plan for each week, each day, and even, perhaps, for each hour that you plan to study. Specific goals will keep you focused so the time you spend in study will be efficient.

√ *Systematic:* In making your study plan, you will need to decide what you want to study, how much time you will spend on each subject/topic, when you wish to build in review, and when you will do practice questions.

√ *Active:* It will be important to self-monitor and self-evaluate as you study. If something is not working well, it will be important to implement a change. Most importantly, you will want to avoid passive, rote methods of study.

Many factors will influence your success in achieving a high score on the USMLE, Step 1.

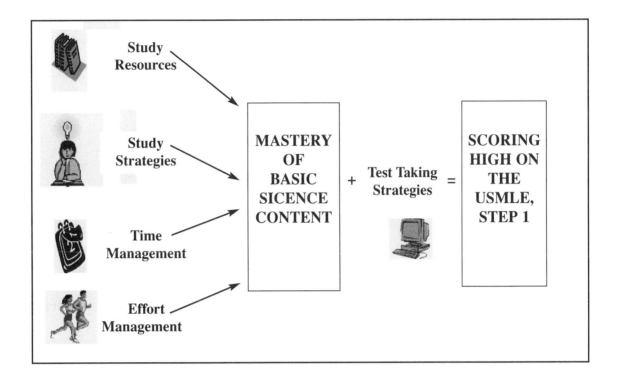

Figure 18.1 Factors to Consider When Preparing for the USMLE, Step 1

As summarized in **Figure 18.1**, Factors to Consider When Preparing for the USMLE, Step 1, you will want to think about:

(1) The *study resources* you will use

(2) The *study strategies* you will implement

(3) How you will schedule your *time*, and

(4) How you will sustain your *effort* in self-directed learning.

You will also want to consider whether your test-taking strategies are effective, since all the information you learn must be effectively applied to answering multiple choice questions on a computerized examination.

1. What Study Resources shall I use?

Choosing materials to use for USMLE review, and using them most effectively, can sometimes be a frustrating experience. You are likely to receive many suggestions from medical students who have already taken the USMLE, Step 1. There are many resources available and each differs in purpose, format, depth and comprehensiveness of content coverage. It is helpful to remember that if there was one book for reviewing a subject that was absolutely "the best," there would not be so many choices of which review books to purchase. You may find materials you have used in the past helpful, especially summary materials you have created yourself.

These guidelines will help you when selecting resources. Three types of study resources are usually needed:

A. Summarized or "compacted" information ("**review books**")

A summarized or compacted review source should provide enough narrative for you to make sense of the topic but not be excessively wordy. It should be able to trigger recall of what you previously learned. These sources are less effective in teaching you something you never learned in the first place. Your own course notes, charts, and handouts are good sources of compacted information. If they were useful to you before, they are likely to be again, as they convey personalized meaning.

B. Questions for self-testing to note progress and to set priorities

It is important to use questions that simulate the format and difficulty of the USMLE, Step 1. There are a number of question books and questions on CD-ROM currently available. When gathering resources, be certain to include questions arranged "topically" (e.g., questions on Cardiovascular Physiology), "composites" by subject or system (e.g., a set of questions on Physiology or a set of Cardiovascular questions), and "mixed composites," the format of questions on the USMLE, Step 1. It is very important to become familiar with the computerized version of the exam by using the questions on the USMLE website (http://www.usmle.org). Remember, these questions are distributed by the National Board of Medical Examiners and therefore are currently the only "official" samples of actual exam questions.

C. Texts (including atlases and other visual materials):

For each of the basic sciences it is useful to identify a textbook that can be used as a reference source, if needed. For example, you may come across some topics in your review book that are not well covered or fully explanatory. You may need to read more comprehensive material in the textbook. How to do effective, selective, focussed reading, was covered in Chapter 2: Acquisition, "Using Your Textbook Effectively."

2. What Study Strategies are best for review and retention?

Study strategies that are relevant when studying for the USMLE have all been discussed in earlier chapters of this book. Some of these strategies and a reminder of their relevance and usefulness are listed here:

1. **Active Learning:** Maintain active learning strategies which are self-directed, aggressive, and monitored. (See Chapter 1: The Basics.)

2. **Setting priorities for review:** It would be comfortable to think about being able to review "everything," but this is not a realistic goal. Begin to determine your priorities by asking:

   A. What are the "important" topics on the USMLE, Step 1?

   B. What are my weak areas?

   C. How did I perform in each of my courses, i.e., What was my initial understanding of the material?

   D. What do I already know? What do I NOT know? *To increase your score on the USMLE, Step 1, it is important to study what you DON'T know and avoid spending time restudying what you already know.*

3. **Reviewing cumulatively and spacing your practice:** This method of review was described in Chapter 4: Maintenance. As you plan your study over several weeks, it will be essential to utilize these principles. For example, if you plan to study Biochemistry during Week 1 of your 4-week study plan, you will also find it useful to review Biochemistry in subsequent weeks. Studying two subjects a day (instead of just one), e.g., Biochemistry in the morning and Behavioral Science in the afternoon, will make it possible for you to "space" your study over more days/weeks. Completing practice questions for self- assessment is an excellent way to both review and to assess knowledge to determine what follow up study is needed.

4. **Self-monitoring:** Remember, one of "The Basics" to effective learning (described in Chapter 1: The Basics) is to maintain an awareness of everything you do. You will particularly want to monitor your attention, concentration, and the effectiveness of your study during preparation for the USMLE, Step 1.

5. **Engaging in self-assessment:** Use questions throughout your study period to identify material you have not yet mastered. Effective preparation for the USMLE involves an on-going process of study, self-assessment, and focussed review based on the results of your assessments. Remember, you

do not have to feel that you have reached "proficiency" to begin questions, as this is a process that can be helpful in deciding what your focus should be, and how effective your test taking strategies are. (See Chapter 4: Proficiency for more details.) Although you are likely to do practice questions from books, be certain to do timed practice questions on a computer as well.

3. How can I best manage my time?

You hopefully will be preparing for the USMLE, Step 1 at a time when you have few other responsibilities. In fact, this may be the longest period of time you will ever spend without other obligations, e.g., course work or clinical duties. However, regardless of how much time you are able to devote to your review, you will probably still end up feeling that you did not have enough time. Therefore, it will be important to develop a long-term study plan. Most students spend 3 to 6 weeks or longer preparing for this important exam. The time management strategies discussed in Chapter 1: The Basics, will continue to be helpful. Be specific in planning your time and remember to build in study breaks.

How to develop a study schedule: The worksheet in **Appendix A** of this chapter will help in this process. Schedules developed and used by students when preparing for the USMLE, Step 1 are included in Appendix B. These are some general principles to follow in making a schedule:

A. First, you must decide how many weeks you will have to prepare for the USMLE, Step 1. It is recommended that you leave 3 to 5 days at the end of your review period just to do questions and very focussed review. Therefore, it is best not to count these days as you develop your study schedule.

B. Be familiar with what subjects will be tested on the USMLE, Step 1. These are listed at the beginning of this chapter. Allocate time to each science and across sciences for integrated study. Set priorities for study based on your own strengths and weaknesses. It is useful to divide subjects or systems into the ones you know fairly well, your *strengths*, those you know *moderately well*, and those you consider to be *weak* ones for you. It will be important to continue to study your strong subjects, as students who ignore these, and study only their weaker areas, seem to end up reversing their areas of strengths and weaknesses. The subjects you know moderately well should be reviewed to make them into your strengths. For those subjects that are weak (perhaps you did not learn them well, or studied them only during your first year of medical school), you may not have time now to learn everything. It is best to review this material *selectively*, beginning with the material that you consider to be high yield, i.e., the most likely topics to be tested. If you have time, you can study other topics that are weak.

C. Decide on time allotment by estimating the number of days you would like to spend reviewing each subject and topic, keeping in mind the total number of days you have allotted for exam review. Use a monthly or weekly calendar to make a schedule.

D. Identify realistic blocks of study time. By the time you are preparing for the USMLE, it is likely you will have a good idea of how much time you are able to concentrate and focus on your study each day, and when you need to take breaks. You will also have an idea of the times of the day that are most and least effective for study (early morning, midday, evening, etc.)

Creating a realistic study schedule will aid in maintaining momentum to complete a comprehensive review of the basic sciences so you feel ready when your exam day arrives.

4. What can I do to sustain effort in studying?

Many strategies (some already discussed in this book) will help to sustain the effort needed for study and to reduce your stress:

1. Select the resources you plan to use before you begin studying, and have them easily accessible. This will allow you to focus just on studying.

2. Select a place to study with few distractions. Since you are likely to be studying over a long period of time, it can be useful to select more than one place. For example, you may wish to spend mornings in one place and afternoons in another; you may wish to have a study place for Mondays, Wednesdays, and Fridays, and another place for other days of the week; or you may wish to have week day/weekend places for study.

3. Plan "guilt free" study breaks. Exercise, and participate in activities you find relaxing. Spend time with your friends. Even short visits are renewing and can help sustain your effort in study. Reward yourself for good effort: Plan a short pleasurable activity each day.

4. Give yourself positive feedback. Practice positive self-talk prior to study and during your study (e.g., "I concentrated well." "I have learned material today that I did not know yesterday."). Maintain awareness of when you have met your study and learning goals.

5. Get enough sleep when studying and sleep well the night before you take the exam. It is best to study during the day and sleep at night, because you will need to be on a day schedule when you take the USMLE, Step 1.

6. Maintain good health. Be certain to eat a healthy diet during your study period. If you get run down, you are more likely to become ill, and you will need to take time to get better. Your study plan will then be compromised.

7. Expect to experience a certain amount of anxiety when preparing for this exam. Managed moderate stress can be helpful in that it will motivate you to follow your study schedule. Unfortunately, with unmanaged high stress, you may have trouble concentrating. It is useful to learn and practice stress management techniques such as meditation, progressive relaxation, and relaxing visual imagery. A counselor from your student wellness program may be able to help with this approach.

5. Test-taking Strategies

Test-taking strategies are discussed in Chapter 4: Proficiency. The following strategies are particularly important when taking the computerized USMLE, Step 1 and should be practiced when taking simulated computer-based questions during your study:

1. Pace yourself. You will have a 1 hour block to answer 50 questions, a little more than a minute per question. (If you finish in less than 1 hour you may leave the block, but may not return to it. Therefore, there is little advantage in rushing through.) Check yourself periodically, but not after each question, to see if you are on time. Then you will be able to speed up or slow down if necessary.

2. Read carefully. Some of the question stems are long so it is best to avoid extensive rereading of questions. Restate the essential information.

3. Carefully analyze each answer choice (T, T?, F, F?, ?), in your head or by using the laminated note board provided for your use during the exam. This method is described in Chapter 4: Proficiency. Although you will most likely not have time to do this written analysis for *all* the questions, it may be an option on the longer questions and the ones that may seem confusing. Mark the questions you would like to return to if you have time. Remember, once you leave a block, you will not be able to return to those questions.

4. Work in sequence but mark the questions you would like to go back to review. Remember: *Change an answer only if you are confident that your original answer is incorrect.*

C.   Frequently Asked Questions

• *Should I take a review course to prepare for the USMLE, Step 1?*

This decision is up to you. Many students decide to take a review course to study for the exam, either one given by their medical school, or a commercial course. However, most students decide to study for the exam on their own. There is no data to suggest that students who take a review course do any better or worse than students who study on their own. Just because you may have taken a review course to prepare for the SAT or MCAT does not mean that you should take a USMLE Board Review course. In making your decision, consider the following:

I should study on my own…

- If I have difficulty learning from lectures.
- If I can't bear to sit in lectures for many hours a day.
- If I have a fairly strong knowledge base, i.e., if I have done well in medical school.
- If I like to make my own decisions on how much time to spend on each subject/topic, to personalize the process so I can spend more time on my weak areas.
- If I have a study partner and/or good support group.

I should take a review course…

- If I know my knowledge base is fairly weak because of borderline grades or having taken basic science courses over an extended period.
- If I want to have all my materials supplied to avoid decisions about what resources I should choose.
- If I need more focus on what is likely to be asked on the exam (high-yield material).
- If I would have difficulty sustaining study on my own.

• *Should I plan my study by subjects (Biochemistry, Physiology, Pathology, etc) or should I take a systems approach (Cardiovascular, Pulmonary, Renal, etc.)?*

This is a decision that should be based on personal preference. Neither approach appears to be superior in terms of achieving higher scores on the USMLE, Step 1. Traditionally, review books have been written for each subject. However, more recently, many review materials take a systems approach. Even if you decide to approach your study by systems, there are still some subjects you will need to approach separately, e.g., Biochemistry, Microbiology and Behavioral Science. Therefore, most students take a combined approach, studying by both systems and subjects as appropriate.

- *When should I begin using questions?*

Complete questions throughout your review. Engaging in on-going self-assessment is important to identify material to review and to practice test taking. When studying for the USMLE, Step 1 it is best to use several types of questions: topical questions, questions that are presented by subjects or by systems, and mixed composite exams, similar in presentation to the USMLE. As you finish studying a topic/subject/system, you may wish to take a set of questions under timed conditions, to simulate the exam. Be sure to do some of your questions on a computer.

- *How many hours a day do I need to spend studying to do well on this exam?*

The amount of time students choose to study each day is highly variable. Some students plan to study 10 to 12 hours per day, but this is likely to be unrealistic, especially since USMLE preparation often takes place over many weeks. A rule of thumb is to plan for a moderate amount of study time, perhaps 7 to 8 hours a day, which includes both brief and longer study breaks. This seems adequate for many students. However, if you are not making the progress you would like, you can easily increase the time you are spending, without undue pressure. Leaving less intensive study activities for the evening hours can sometimes be helpful. For example, students often do questions in the evenings, or study a subject that is less difficult for them, or review previously studied material.

- *How should I schedule my study breaks? How much break time should I take?*

Frequent breaks to maintain active learning are important. Often students find it helpful to take a 5 to 10 minute short break every hour, a 1 to 2 hour break at midday, and a break before dinner. It is also recommended that you set aside at least one day a week to relax. This "day" can be taken all at once or spread into two or more time slots during the week. For example, some students like to take off Friday evening, Saturday evening and Sunday morning. Others like to take off Saturday afternoon and evening, and Sunday morning. Your decision as to when and how long to study will be a personal one based on your preference and needs.

Best wishes for wonderful success on the USMLE!

Appendix A: Planning Worksheet for the USMLE, Step 1

The following worksheet will be helpful when you are ready to develop your study plan for the USMLE, Step 1:

USMLE, STEP 1: DEVELOPING A STUDY PLAN

1. What is your test date? _____ How many days do you have to study after your classes and exams are over?_____ Now subtract 3 to 5 days._____

   It is recommended that this is the actual number of days you should plan your review. The last several days will be spent doing questions and engaging in selective/focussed review.

2. Make a list of the subjects you need to review for this exam in priority order, beginning with the ones you feel you remember LEAST well. If you are still taking basic science courses, your current courses will likely be your areas of strength by the time you are preparing to study for the exam.

3. Have you made a decision to review subject by subject (Anatomy, Biochemistry, Physiology, etc.) or by systems (Cardiovascular, Respiratory, Renal, etc.)? Are you planning a combined approach? What are the reasons for your decision?

4. Deciding on time allotment: Take a look at the list you created under #2. Estimate the number of days you would like to review each topic/subject within the time constraints that you have. This will be helpful even if you have decided to proceed with a systems approach. Consider the following:

   A. The total number of study days must add up to the number of days you will have.

   B. Some time each day will be spent reviewing material you have previously studied.

   C. You will be taking breaks.

   Now transfer this information to a monthly calendar.

5. Next, begin to transfer your time estimates onto a weekly/hourly schedule. It is recommended that you use pencil as schedules are apt to change, and only do this kind of detailed planning one week at a time. Keep in mind the rules about taking breaks.

You now have a study plan!

Appendix B: Sample Study Schedules

Each of these students has created a schedule based on personal strengths, weaknesses and preferences. The schedules are included here as examples, not as models to be copied. It is best to develop a study schedule prior to beginning to study for the USMLE, Step 1. Develop a schedule that meets your individual needs, but do not agonize over the one best schedule (which likely does not exist.) Remember to set priorities, review comprehensively, self-monitor and prepare to make changes along the way.

All three schedules, although **not explicitly** indicated, have the following in common:

1. Comprehensive review of basic science, but no attempt to review everything.

2. A combination of subject and system review.

3. On-going cumulative review and spaced practice.

4. Use of questions throughout (study-test-follow up).

5. Distinct period (3 to 5 days) before the exam day devoted to mixed composite questions and focussed review.

6. Some time to relax the day before taking the exam.

1. Student A will take a Systems/Subject Approach over a 4-week period. Twenty-three days are scheduled for review and 5 days are left for question sets and focussed review. Biochemistry, studied during the first semester of medical school, will be reviewed first. Behavioral Science, a current course with an NBME Subject Test final exam, will be reviewed briefly in three evenings.

System or Subject	Time
Biochemistry	5 days
Cardiovascular*	4 days
Pulmonary*	3 days
Renal*	3 days
GI*	2 days
Endocrine*	1 day
Immunology/Hematology	2 days
Neuroscience	1 day
Microbiology	2 days
Behavioral Science	3 evenings (9 hours)
Embryology	2 evenings (4 hours)
Questions	Throughout
Composite Question Sets & Focussed Review	5 days

*Study of these systems includes: Anatomy, Physiology, Histology, Pathology, Pharmacology

2. Student B plans a Systems/Subject Approach for 27 days. An intense course (Biochemistry) will be studied in conjunction with Behavioral Science. A full-day break after the first week is planned. Microbiology, a course requiring memorization, is scheduled for Days 21 and 22.

Day 1	Biochemistry & Behavioral Science	Day 13	Immunology & Hematology
2	Biochemistry & Behavioral Science	14	Break
3	Biochemistry & Behavioral Science	15	GI*
4	Biochemistry & Embryology	16	GI*
5	Biochemistry & Embryology	17	Endocrine & Reproductive*
6	Cell Biology & Neuroscience	18	Endocrine*
7	Break	19	Renal*
8	Cardiovascular*	20	Renal*
9	Cardiovascular*	21	Microbiology
10	Pulmonary*	22	Microbiology
11	Pulmonary*	23-27	Questions & Review
12	Immunology & Hematology	28	USMLE, Step 1

*Study of these systems includes: Anatomy, Physiology, Histology, Pathology, Pharmacology

3. Student C has planned another version of a Systems/Subject approach, over a 31-day period. One day will be scheduled for Microbiology in each of the last 3 weeks.

System or Subject	Time
Biochemistry	3 1/2 days
Cardiovascular*	4 1/2 days
Respiratory*	3 1/2 days
Renal*	3 1/2 days
GI*	2 1/2days
Microbiology	3 days
Neuroscience	2 days
Endocrine*	1 day
Questions & Focussed Review	4 1/2 days
Behavioral Science	Throughout

*Study of these systems includes: Anatomy, Physiology, Histology, Pathology, Pharmacology

The next step for these students, is to write the schedule on a monthly calendar and then on a daily calendar, indicating study time, when the questions and review are scheduled, and when breaks are planned. Student C has filled in the schedule as shown on the calendar in **Figure 18.2**.

It is helpful to take note of these features:

• Study activities are scheduled for morning, afternoon and evening.

• Evening hours are often left for completing questions, reviewing, or reading Behavioral Science, a less taxing subject for this student.

• Breaks are scheduled every week, including the day before the examination.

May and June

Sunday	Moonday	Tuesday	Wednesday	Thursday	Friday	Saturday
Key **Q**=Questions **R**=Review **CV**=Cardio. Sys.	**Resp**=Resp. Sys. **Anat**=Gross Anat. & Embryol.		**8** Last Medical School Exam	**9** BREAK	**10** AM Biochemistry PM Biochemistry EVE BREAK	**11** AM Biochemistry PM Biochemistry EVE Q-Biochem
12 BREAK (MOTHER'S DAY)	**13** AM Biochemistry PM Biochemistry EVE Q-Biochem	**14** AM Biochemistry PM CV Anat Embryo. EVE Biochem Rev Questions	**15** AM CV Physio PM CV Physio EVE Q CV Physio	**16** AM CV Physio PM CV Path EVE Behavioral Science	**17** AM CV Path PM CV Path EVE Q CV Path R	**18** AM CV Pharm PM CV Pharm EVE BREAK
19 AM Microbiology PM Microbiology EVE Resp. Anat. Embryo	**20** AM Resp. Physio PM Resp. Physio EVE Q Resp. Physio CV Composite	**21** AM Resp. Histo Path PM Resp Path EVE Q Resp Path R	**22** AM Resp Pharm PM Resp Pharm EVE Q Resp Composite R	**23** AM Renal Anat Physio PM Renal Physio EVE Q Renal Physio R	**24** AM Renal Path PM Renal Path EVE BREAK	**25** AM Renal Path PM Renal Pharm EVE BREAK
26 AM BREAK PM Renal Pharm EVE Renal Composite R	**27** AM Microbiology PM Microbiology EVE Microbiology R	**28** AM Neuroscience PM Neuroscience EVE Q Neuroscience R	**29** AM Neuroscience PM Neuroscience EVE Neuro R	**30** AM GI, Anat, Physio PM GI, Physio EVE Beh. Science	**30** AM GI, Anat, Physio PM GI, Physio EVE Q, CV, Resp, Renal	**1** AM GI, PM GI Ques EVE BREAK
2 AM BREAK or R PM Q Biochem, Neuro EVE R	**3** AM Endocrine PM Endocrine EVE Q Endocrine Q Beh Sci	**4** AM Microbiol PM Microbiol EVE Q Micro R	**5** Composite Questions and Focussed High Yield Review	**6** Composite Questions and Focussed High Yield Review	**7** Composite Questions and Focussed High Yield Review	**8** Composite Questions and Focussed High Yield Review
9 AM R PM BREAK EVE BREAK	**10** **Test Day USMLE, Step 1**					

Figure 18.2

Notes

The popular First Edition of

How to Excel in Medical School

was adopted by the following educational institutions:

University of Vermont Medical School
University of Puerto Rico Medical School
Ohio College of Podiatric Medicine
University of Medicine and Dentistry of New Jersey
New Jersey Medical School
University of Mississippi Medical Center
Northeastern Ohio Universities College of Medicine
Charles R. Drew University
University of Massachusetts Memorial Health Center
Tuskegee University
University of Missouri-Kansas City Medical Center
Rutgers University
Wayne State University School of Medicine
West Virginia School of Osteopathic Medicine
University of Michigan